THE 12 ANGULAR POINTS OF SOCIAL JUSTICE AND PEACE

BOOKS BY PETER FRITZ WALTER

CREATIVE-C LEARNING: THE INNOVATIVE KINDERGARTEN

TAO TE CHING (ENGLISH AND GERMAN TRANSLATIONS)

DAS DAO DER STAATSFÜHRUNG UND STRATEGIE (GERMAN)

ÉCRITS POÉTIQUES (FRENCH)

ESSAYS ON LAW, POLICY, AND PSYCHIATRY (14 VOLUMES)

EVIDENCE AND BURDEN OF PROOF IN SOVEREIGN IMMUNITY LITIGATION: A PROCEDURAL GUIDE FOR INTERNATIONAL LAWYERS AND GOVERNMENT COUNSEL (DOCTORAL THESIS)

GREAT MINDS SERIES (11 VOLUMES)

INTEGRATE YOUR EMOTIONS: A GUIDE TO EMOTIONAL WHOLENESS

LITIGATION PRACTICE AND BURDEN OF PROOF UNDER THE FOREIGN SOVEREIGN IMMUNITIES ACT, 1976: A PROCEDURAL GUIDE FOR INTERNATIONAL LAWYERS IN THE UNITED STATES AND CANADA

POETIC WRITINGS 1990-2010 (STORIES, PAMPHLETS, POEMS, ESSAYS)

POETISCHE SCHRIFTEN (GERMAN)

SCHOLARLY ARTICLES (21 VOLUMES)

SHAMANIC WISDOM MEETS THE WESTERN MIND

THE 12 ANGULAR POINTS OF SOCIAL JUSTICE AND PEACE

THE BETTER LIFE: TRANSFORMING YOURSELF FROM INSIDE OUT

THE ENERGY NATURE OF HUMAN EMOTIONS AND SEXUAL ATTRACTION: A SYSTEMIC ANALYSIS OF EMOTIONAL IDENTITY IN THE PROCESS OF THE HUMAN SEXUAL RESPONSE

THE LEADERSHIP I CHING: YOUR DAILY COMPANION FOR PRACTICAL GUIDANCE

THE NEW PARADIGM SERIES (BOOK REVIEWS, 3 VOLUMES)

THE VIBRANT NATURE OF LIFE: A SCIENCE-BASED PATHWAY FOR A BETTER, RICHER, AND MORE ABUNDANT LIFE

WALTER'S CAREER AND LEADERSHIP SERIES (3 VOLUMES)

THE 12 ANGULAR POINTS OF SOCIAL JUSTICE AND PEACE

SOCIAL POLICY FOR THE 21ST CENTURY

by Peter Fritz Walter

Published by Sirius-C Media Galaxy LLC

113 Barksdale Professional Center, Newark, Delaware, USA

Set in Palatino

Designed by Peter Fritz Walter

ISBN 978-1-515143-51-2

Publishing Categories
Nonfiction / Social Science / Violence in Society

Publisher Contact Information
publisher@sirius-c-publishing.com
http://sirius-c-publishing.com

Author Contact Information
pfw@peterfritzwalter.com

About Dr. Peter Fritz Walter
http://peterfritzwalter.com

About the Author

Parallel to an international law career in Germany, Switzerland and the United States, Dr. Peter Fritz Walter (Pierre) focused upon fine art, cookery, astrology, musical performance, social sciences and humanities.

He started writing essays as an adolescent and received a high school award for creative writing and editorial work for the school magazine.

After finalizing his law diplomas, he graduated with an LL.M. in European Integration at Saarland University, Germany, in 1982, and with a Doctor of Law title from University of Geneva, Switzerland, in 1987.

He then took courses in psychology at the University of Geneva and interviewed a number of psychotherapists in Lausanne and Geneva, Switzerland. His interest was intensified through a hypnotherapy with an Ericksonian American hypnotherapist in Lausanne. This led him to the recovery and healing of his inner child.

After a second career as a corporate trainer and personal coach, Pierre retired in 2004 as a full-time writer, philosopher and consultant.

His nonfiction books emphasize a systemic, holistic, cross-cultural and interdisciplinary perspective, while his fiction works and short stories focus upon education, philosophy, perennial wisdom, and the poetic formulation of an integrative worldview.

Pierre is a German-French bilingual native speaker and writes English as his 4th language after German, Latin and French. He also reads source literature for his research works in Spanish, Italian, Portuguese, and Dutch. In addition, Pierre has notions of Thai, Khmer, Chinese, Japanese, and Vietnamese.

All of Pierre's books are hand-crafted and self-published, designed by the author. Pierre publishes via his Delaware company, Sirius-C Media Galaxy LLC, and under the imprints of IPUBLICA and SCM (Sirius-C Media).

There is no good that is always or only good, no single virtue appropriate to every situation. Lao-tzu tells us that it is only when we lose contact with out innate intuitive intelligence that we resort to 'goodness' and 'righteousness' as the ethical guideposts of our lives. It is only when real love is lost that we resort to 'filial piety' or 'family values.' It is in this spirit that we can understand St. Thomas Aquinas' dictum, 'Love God and do as you please.' Love is superior to any ethical code.

—LAURENCE G. BOLD IN THE TAO OF ABUNDANCE (1999)

The classical Taoists take a much more positive view of human nature. For the Taoist, all depraved or perverse manifestations of human behavior result from rejecting our deepest nature, not from following it. It is by denying the unity of all life and committing to the attachment of the ego that we go astray.

—LAURENCE G. BOLD IN THE TAO OF ABUNDANCE (1999)

Insofar as love expresses itself, it is not expressing itself in terms of the socially approved manners of life. That's why it is all so secret. Love has nothing to do with social order.

—JOSEPH CAMPBELL IN THE POWER OF MYTH (1988)

The author's profits from this book are being donated to charity.

Contents

Overview

The 12 Angular Points

01/12 — Harmless Wrongdoing

The 'Making' of Crime fosters Social Conflict.
Decriminalizing Harmless Human Behavior Fosters Social Peace.

02/12 — The Possible Human

Possible Humans are the Rule.
Impossible Citizens are the Exceptions from the Rule.

03/12 — Fostering Public Sanity

Public Sanity is Public Mental Hygiene.
Republic Insanity is Absence of Governmental Hygiene.

04/12 — Respecting Natural Intimacy

Natural Intimacy is Conducive to Peace.
Governmental Intimidation is Conducive to Civil War.

05/12 — Serving Children

From Protecting Children to Serving Children.
Free Choice Relations for Children.

06/12 — More Public Education

More Public Education Makes for Less Crime.
More Prison Miles Make for More Crime.

07/12—Free Education

Free Education Serves the Child.
Funded Disinformation Serves State Control Over the Child.

08/12—Politically Neutral Science

Politically Neutral Science Promotes Truth.
Politically Correct Science Promotes Ideology.

09/12—Humanism and Realism

Humanism and Realism is Objective Perception.
Idealism and Ideology is Distorted Perception.

10/12—Promoting Pleasure-Seeking Behaviors

Promoting the Pleasure Function Reduces Violence.
Condemning Pleasure as Negative Morality Raises Violence.

11/12—Male Affection as a Peace Conductor

Homoemotional Affection gets Males into Balance.
Homosexual Attraction gets Males out of Balance.

12/12—Fostering Permissive Education

Promoting the Cause of the Sexual Child is not Pedophilia.
Pedophilia is Not a Cause but a Psychosexual Hangup.

01/12

Harmless Wrongdoing

The 'Making' of Crime fosters Social Conflict.
Decriminalizing Harmless Human Behavior Fosters Social Peace.

It has become *almost a fashion* among governments around the world to legally declare as *'criminal'* forms of behavior that are simply natural and that typically were unregulated as long as human habitat was closer to nature, and less technologized.

—See, for example, Joel Feinberg, Harmless Wrongdoing: The Moral Limits of the Criminal Law (1990).

This trend that after all must be seen as a form of *legislative perversion* started in the 1970s and 80s with declaring the ingestion of certain plants illegal, such as hemp (cannabis), psychedelic mushrooms and shrubs, else substances that, while being artificially produced such as LSD are *conducive to altering states of consciousness*, and that were widely used in psychiatry and transformative psychology.

—See, for example, Richard Schultes, et. al, Plants of the Gods (2002), Albert Hofmann, LSD, My Problem Child (1980/2009), Michael Harner, Ways of the Shaman (1980/1982), Holger Kalweit, Shamans, Healers and Medicine Men ((1987/2000), Jeremy Narby, The Cosmic

Serpent (1999), Terence McKenna, Food of the Gods (1992), Stanislav Grof, LSD: Doorway to the Numinous (1975/2009) and The Cosmic Game (1998), as well as Rick Strassman, DMT, The Spirit Molecule (2001). See also Ralph Metzner (Ed.), Ayahuasca (1999), Robert Forte (Ed.), Entheogens and the Future of Religion (1997) and Charles T. Tart (Ed.), Altered States of Consciousness (1969).

Albert Hofmann, from *Sandoz Laboratories,* Switzerland, and discoverer of LSD, wrote in his book *LSD: My Problem Child (1979/2009),* p. 15:

LSD researchers responded in different ways to the legal and political sanctions against psychedelics. Some of them grudgingly accepted them and reluctantly returned to mainstream therapeutic practices, which now seemed to them boring and painfully ineffective. A few of us attempted to develop non-drug methods for inducing non-ordinary states of consciousness with the experiential spectrum and healing potential comparable to psychedelics. There were also those who saw the extraordinary benefits of LSD psychotherapy and decided not to sacrifice the wellbeing of their clients to irrational and scientifically unsubstantiated legislation, and continued their work in secret. In addition to the therapeutic value of psychedelics, many of these professionals were also aware of the entheogenic potential of these substances. For this reason, they understood their work with LSD to be not only therapeutic practice, but also religious activity in the best sense of the word. From this perspective, the legal sanctions against psychedelics appeared to be not only unfounded and misguided, but represented a

serious infringement of religious freedom guaranteed by the American Constitution.

Stanislav Grof, M.D., the most experienced psychiatrist and maverick researcher on LSD psychotherapy, writes in *LSD: Doorway to the Numinous (1975/2009)*, Preface, p. xxv. on the therapeutic value of LSD:

> The unique property of psychedelics makes it possible to study psychological undercurrents that govern our experiences and behaviors to a depth that cannot be matched by any other method or tool available in mainstream psychiatry and psychology. In addition, it offers unique opportunities for healing of emotional and psychosomatic disorders, for positive personality transformation, and for consciousness evolution.

Ralph Metzner writes in the introduction to his bestselling *Ayahuasca Reader (1999)* that those plants 'are referred to as medicines, a term that means more than a drug: something like a healing power or energy that can be associated with a plant, a person, an animal, even a place, and that [t]hey are also referred to as plant teachers. Lester Grinspoon, M.D. reports in his well-researched book *Marihuana: The Forbidden Medicine (1997)* that back in 1621, the English clergyman Robert Burton, in his reputed

workbook *The Anatomy of Melancholy,* 'suggested the use of cannabis in the treatment of depression.'

He also notes that once Marihuana had become 'the forbidden medicine,' '[m]ore than a thousand people die from aspirin-induced bleeding each year in the United States, and barbiturates are, of course, far more dangerous.'

As Terence McKenna once observed, *declaring nature illegal* borders mental and governmental insanity!

This trend was then expanding to declare natural child sexuality a form of *criminal behavior,* with the result that children and adolescents from the age of twelve who engage in sexual behavior with peers are labeled as *sex offenders* and are convicted and registered on public sex offender registries. This results in their later careers being jeopardized, if they do not suffer one or the other form of lynch justice! To get there legally despite paying lip service to *child protection* was possible only by once again declaring nature insane and culture sane, namely by legally forging the concept of *child sexual abuse* and simply expanding the concept of *sex offender* from applying it

to adults, to applying it equally to youngsters and children.

It is really demonic as a governmental behavior, and social and legal policy making, to get to this point of *legislative perversion* when you figure that the concept of 'child sexual abuse' was forged for protecting children from abuse, not for declaring children themselves as abusers.

The rationale behind this policy making is that there is no rationale, but an *irrationale*. The irrational and mythic delusion behind this behavior is a blunt imitation of Church Rules during the Middle-Ages where suspiciously so, the abuse victim was always blamed for having let it happen, and typically, the Church was burning the raped child together with the rapist, on one and the same stake!

Hence, these new social and legal policies that label children as sex offenders are by no means forms of rational social and legal policy making, and besides, they are simply unconstitutional, and against all human rights conventions. They could be considered as a form of torture under the *United Nations Conventions Against Torture*.

Besides, crime prevention is *much more important* than criminal prosecution. In a sense, prosecution is always too late, just as sex education of children is always too late. In this sense and under such circumstances, prosecution actually becomes persecution!

The state is wise that knows *how to prevent crime* and not the state that has crime happening all over the place and always comes *as it were in the last minute* to make undone what has been done, and to console and comfort the victims.

Countless prison miles are not a solution, human potential lost by incarcerating people for decades is not a solution, it is a *fake solution!* Why? It is no solution because nobody is served. People are destroyed and the tax payer pays the bill for this destruction of human potential; the state is not served either because of the expenses for an *enormously complex administration apparatus* which entails a blown-up budget for law enforcement. In addition, the community is certainly not served by losing so much accumulated human potential! And what about the victims in all the cases the state was too late to prevent the crime? Another casualty?

To ask such a question sounds like cynicism, but is not. It is a matter-of-fact assessment. We really must find effective solutions for crime prevention that are based on the *understanding of human nature,* and the true understanding of human emotions, the sexual function, and the dynamics in human relationships.

We cannot make effective laws when we disregard psychology; if we do that, we get what we have now, a blown-up apparatus that looks like a *huge state bulldog* that has the intelligence of a Neanderthal brain.

The real solution is *crime prevention through smart social policy making.* I mean by this not just legal policy making, not just lawmaking but *changing social structures long-term,* and guiding citizens to constructive forms of behavior. We cannot effectively reduce psychopathological and antisocial behaviors *by punishing those behaviors.*

The system of 'punishment and reward' simply doesn't work with humans, while it may work with dogs and monkeys. The patriarchal way doesn't work either. It has disqualified itself over the last *five thousand years of total madness!*

Changing behaviors is a long-term endeavor and it can only succeed when it is based upon a correct assessment of the human nature. This is the crucial point, as I show it in all my publications. We need to get away from *century-old projections upon the human nature* to really finding out about new solutions by observing living systems and through understanding the dynamics of human communication.

To give an example, when we ponder how to *bring about positive, non-harmful and constructive sexual behaviors,* we need to study the true nature of human sexuality. When we apply the reductionist and mechanistic science of sexology, we learn that there are *sexual drives,* and that people are conditioned in childhood to follow certain sexual attractions; there is a theory that goes from an ideal scenario saying 'this is the way it should,' and then derives conclusions from this assumption for all the cases that are not going 'as it should,' that is, paraphilias and perversions.

But sexology and depth psychology to this day have not proven the assumption that there *is* really something like 'normal sexual behavior' except there is one striking element in normalcy, in all normal sexual behaviors: it is the *sharing of pleasure.*

Pathological sexual behavior by contrast is characterized by shared pleasure being replaced by *one-sided pleasure inflicted on the mate,* and that uses violent means to achieve satisfaction, virtually 'on the back' of the mate.

My thirty-years research on human sexual behavior, human emotions and sexual paraphilias shows that prior to the sexual response, there is an *emotional bonding,* which is based on what I call 'emotional predilection.' I mean that sexual mating is *not random with human beings,* but typically a result of *emotional bonding* which follows certain emotional patterns.

People are attracted to certain groups of potential mates, such as partners of the opposite sex of a certain age group, partners of same-sex of a certain age group or younger partners of a certain age group. Hence, emotional patterning is depending on *emotional identity,* which is part of general identity. People tend to identify themselves with their emotional patterns, their emotional predilections.

Let us now have a look how sexual behaviors can occur that fall outside of the socially accepted schema.

Why does a man or woman want to work with children and become an educator? Because they feel emotionally attracted to children. Why does a man or a woman want to work for the elderly? Because they are emotionally attracted to elders. Now, in one or the other case, with one or the other person, we have incidents of such kind of professionals having sexual relations with some of the children or elders they care for. What is interesting in these cases is that their pedophilic or gerontophilic emotions turned sexual.

While for a majority of those workers, it did not happen, it happened with them. And while even with them, they did not feel such kind of erotic attraction to all children or elders, they felt it for *some of them.*

How can that happen? My hypothesis is that the children or the elders *gave the signal* for the relationship, as unusual as it may sound, given the fact that educational and therapeutic relations are deemed to be *nonsexual,* and that the worker could not cope with that projection and accordingly was trapped without actually cognizing the entanglement —until it was too late!

Now, if we register this and accept this to happen, because moralizing would sidetrack us in our rational

analysis of such events, what comes next? We should wonder *why we are not giving some kind of preparative training* to workers to anticipate such kind of accidents? This has to my knowledge never been done and that is why I suggest to set this up, as a special branch within educators' vocational training.

The answer to this question is that we did not know that the etiology of sexual attraction is not sexual, but *emotional.* That is why we thought that when such a case occurred, the worker in question was 'premeditating' a sexual attack long before and staged everything for the purpose of an 'intended abuse.'

Such is the official rhetoric, such is the cunning way our legal system rules out any other etiology, because the 'premeditation theory' simply fits ideally into the 'abuse-centered culture' with its *simplistic scheme of predators and victims.* And of course, interrogations are led with the 'perpetrators' by police and judges in a way to confirm that the plot was 'premeditated long in advance.'

That things are not that way in most cases doesn't interest anybody, because everybody makes money in such affairs—except those who are trapped by them,

the workers and educators, and of course the children and their parents.

Here are the steps to be taken to change this legal and social paradigm:

—Decriminalize nonviolent consenting adult-child relations. Abolish all sex laws for they do not fit into a modern legal system and are more abusive than all the abuses they are intend to punish;

—Treat dependency relations and tutelary relations basically on the same level, but embed educational relations into the ethical code of the particular organization or school;

—Give children who suffer from physically or sexually abusive parents appropriate shelter and education but allow them to see their parents at regular intervals if they wish to, and do not prohibit parents to visit the children, thereby respecting the internal bond that despite abuse needs continuity for the child to develop his or her psychosexual growth.

In addition, there are manifest constitutional reasons for a change of this situation, which is simply shameful for any nation that says it follows the rule of law and is democratic. Fact is that in most cases involving *child sexual abuse,* the rule in the United

States of America and most other Western nations today is that prosecution proceeds on mere *hearsay* for arresting suspects without any evidence, and with the additional right of the state to take children out of their families, and put them in state custody. Evidence if at all present in these cases, is not primary evidence, but secondary evidence, that is *hearsay or mere suspicion,* or the vague allegations of neighbors about 'suspicious behavior,' which in most cases is so general that virtually everything can be subsumed under it. Even the *Magna Carta* of 1215 was more liberal and granted more protection for the individual, hundreds of years ago, than today's American criminal justice. Hence, in most of these cases we have a flagrant violation of the constitutional principle of *nulla poena sine lege* or *due process.*

Due Process is a a *supreme constitutional principle,* which says that 'nobody can be subjected to a criminal trial without there existing a written law in precise wording prior to the act committed, and under which the behavior in question can be subsumed.

Due process and other constitutional rights have been written in the constitution of the United States by the United States Bill or Rights, which has actually

been added to the constitution in the form of the Ten Amendments. It's a *superior principle in a democracy* for in totalitarian regimes typically people *are condemned by laws that either do not exist or that are applied against their precise wording,* or by extending their wording, so as to have people disappear from the political agenda.

If a democracy is genuine, there typically is a Constitutional Court to monitor the legal system for making sure that constitutional guarantees be applied and safeguarded by all involved in the law profession, including the lawmaker. In the United States, for example, this court is the *United States Supreme Court.*

In Germany, this court is called *Bundesverfassungsgericht,* translated as *German Constitutional Court.* This highest and most respected court of Germany has the power to invalidate laws by force of its adjudicative power.

It has in continued jurisprudence, since its creation in 1942, emphasized the principle of *nulla poena* as a primal constitutional right of the citizen that the state has to comply with by drafting precise criminal laws, those namely that are worded in a way to be *unambiguous and verifiable.*

For example, if *rape* is defined as the *'penetration of the female sexual organ by the male sexual organ'* and in the case at court, the accused penetrated the vagina of the victim by means of a vibrator, the judge in that case would not be allowed to admit rape, because 'vibrator' is not 'male sexual organ' and in criminal law, precisely because of the principle of *nulla poena*, an interpretation and extension of the statute is *not allowed!*

The *German Constitutional Court* has repeatedly invalidated, and thus rendered *null und nichtig* (legally void) legal bills that had passed the *Bundestag* (German Parliament) and that were thus declared to be invalid laws. Because these criminal laws were too general in their wording and not precise enough, they violated the principle of *nulla poena sine lege* that is according to the German Constitutional Court not just a matter of law history, but has *immediate* constitutional validity. As a result, the laws have been nullified by the court and the persons condemned under these laws were *at once liberated from prison and financially compensated for the injustice done to them.* In addition, it has to be seen that the principle of *nulla poena* bears high political and social explosiveness in

the application and extensive interpretation of so-called *sex laws.*

Sex laws are for the most part very *vague* and contain chewing-gum clauses such as, for example, the term 'public morals.' It is for this and other reasons that they have been considered by many constitutional lawyers as violating constitutional law.

In addition, their *extensive* interpretation by criminal jurisprudence in the United States and other jurisdictions makes decidedly for the *unconstitutionality* of these laws, as I have shown in several of my publications and audio books.

I am saying that if the human being today is rampantly engaging in destructive behaviors, the culprit for this fact is exactly governments that form wrong social policies, such as *tolerating outdated 'sex laws'* that bring only evil results, while they are very little effective in a positive sense, that is, in the sense they are deemed to be made for. But they are in fact not made for functioning in our society for they were made by the Church in times of the 'dark age,' as a means of tightly oppressing the population, as a means of control and religious tyranny. It is irresponsible for any modern government to uphold

these laws, and it is naive to think *they were doing any good* in the sense of positive child protection.

They don't, and the evidence is on the table!

Proposal 1/12

My suggestion is to *decriminalize* behavior as much as possible.

LSD should be made available for research as it was effected in 2007, in Switzerland. Marihuana is not a 'hard drug' and its effects are lesser harmful than the effects of alcoholic beverage.

In Holland and Spain every citizen is allowed to have a maximum of four Cannabis plants.

Legalizing drugs leads to the eradication of black markets and reduces crime that is related to those markets. Marihuana is smoked by monks in Nepal for religious purposes. Hemp was used since centuries for healing, especially when brewed as a tea.

—See Lester Grinspoon, Marihuana: The Forbidden Medicine (1997).

The abolishment of age of consent laws and other 'sex laws' is a *matter of rational and responsible policymaking*.

Human sexuality is not damaging anybody, except perhaps the 'morals' of sexually incompetent people whose mindset is pervaded by myths, by fear, and by what I call 'religious perversion,' which is a thinking

where all in life, and especially all the vital life functions, are seen through 'upside-down' glasses.

Such a policy change would give tremendous trust to humans to not being sexually abusive but *live their sexual relations in a responsible manner* that does no harm. The present laws *do not make a significant distinction,* in their punishing sexual abuse of a child, between violent and nonviolent sex with a child. This is so because the fines for violence used are not significantly higher than those for nonviolent sexual play with a child.

That means there is *no stimulus* from such laws for humans to be nonviolent; in the contrary, those laws make for *more violence.*

Without such laws there would be a tremendous stimulus to seek out *consenting relations* with all members of the community.

At the same time children should be empowered to live their sex lives with *peers or adults other than their parents,* as their free choice, and without being emotionally manipulated as it is the case under the present situation of the law and 'social morality.' Besides that, these laws are outdated and irrational as they are the successors of the Church's *Canon Law,* a

body of *ecclesiastical rules* not to be considered by the modern legislator as rational and democratic lawmaking.

Thus, there are several heavy reasons for a future legislator to *eventually abandon these ungainly laws altogether,* and to replace them by competent and responsible sociopsychiatric consultancy that is carried out, as a state function, by state-trusted consultancy agencies.

02/12

The Possible Human

Possible Humans are the Rule.
Impossible Citizens are the Exceptions from the Rule.

The general trend in the *Aquarius Age* will be away
from collectivism and toward individualism, away
from standard opinions and rules toward more
freedom for setting and living one's own personalized
standards and ways of life. The regard of the state
upon the citizen will largely shift. While within the
authoritarian if not totalitarian state of the Pisces Age,
the citizen was a subject, for the democratic Aquarian
state, the citizen is a customer.

The *Aquarius Age* shall provide the individual with
a greater sphere of self-expression and more options
for associating with peers and groupings that pursue
similar goals, even in the case that those goals may be
different from the opinions or the lifestyle of the
average individual, or the majority.

There will definitely be more space and
recognition for alternative lifestyles.

The influence of social and political bodies over the individual will decrease and become smoother.

Without being blurred by our great philosophies that more often than not have justified violence and injustice with grandiose slogans, we will come to understand that most governments are inspired in their evildoing against their citizens by something called 'the human nature.' Through the terrible mix of religious doctrine, misunderstood for the most part, together with distorted political ideas, we got nowhere, collectively, in our task for understanding the human being, while there are of course many intelligent, far-sighted and integer humans who have the right vision, and who have written wonderful books.

But collectively, on the government level of our glorious civilizations, embodied in our nation states, what we see is the grossest misevaluation of human nature that one can possibly imagine. Most governments, in their overall approach toward their citizens, even today, are taking for granted the Calvinist belief that the 'human soul is rotten and the flesh weak,' and that without 'punishment and reward,' humans would behave in criminal and chaotic ways; this is why, under the header of

moralism, the upside-down concept of genuine morality, so much violence and oppression are inflicted upon the 'impossible human.'

The human race was not always violent, and violence is not something mysterious and fatal we have to accept; much to the contrary, the roots of violence have been elucidated by an *abundance of research* over the last fifty years or so. We have today massive evidence for the fact that contrary to the beliefs of fundamentalist religions, homo sapiens is not violent by nature. Historical and anthropological research shows that most of the pre-patriarchal cultures were peaceful and nonviolent.

In the social history of our own society, however, and at a time when it was unknown how important sensuality is in nutritive child-rearing, laws and policies were drafted that atrociously punished people for being naturally sensual with a child, or for giving a child tactile stimulation in the form of caresses, kisses, tender fondling and by licking the child's skin.

But this changed since the 1960s and 70s, when neurology, anthropology and skin research coincided in showing that one of the surest factors in the

etiology of violence is emotional and tactile deprivation of infants, children and adolescents through insufficient or inadequate nursing.

Today, it is without a doubt established doctrine in psychology, education and the mental health professions that tactile stimulation and emotionally abundant and empathetic parenting is one of the ways to reduce violence both domestically and structurally.

These strategies should be endorsed, supported and encouraged by governments.

Only very recently there is a fundamental shift to be noted in a paradigm that lasted over the whole of patriarchy. This paradigm could be called a negative worldview. This negative worldview prevailed since the last five thousand years or so, and was particularly negative regarding nature and human nature.

This paradigm assumed that the human is a dangerous mix between some 'good' and a lot of 'bad' drives or instincts and that those latter instincts had to be kept in check. There was a particular stress upon morality and education, for reforming the presumed 'impossible human' into something better. As a result,

moralism prevailed over most of human history and was widely justified with the need to safeguard 'law and order' by holding the 'bad citizen' in a tight corset of legal and social prohibitions and taboos.

I have written the present book because I believe that proactive policy making means to change the reigning group fantasy from the 'impossible' to the 'possible' human.

This implies updating our retarded notion of the human being as a 'biologically violent creature' that was promoted by decrepit theories like social Darwinism and by all our religions that found never anything good about the human, while they were and are completely unaware that by doing so they all are liable of blasphemy.

Religions are thus out of the game, and to be disqualified for any input in social policy making because they have never walked their talk. While they praise the Creator, they basically say that His Creation is faulty and 'has to be improved,' thereby arrogating themselves to know better than the Creator. This is simply blasphemic, was it not simply ridiculous after all! The results of this group fantasy, however, are

quite serious, in the form of projections being made upon the human nature that inherently are not there.

This was done so over the whole course of patriarchy, the last 5000 years, but it was only detected as fraud or 'flawed reasoning' since about the last two decades, namely with the advent of systems theory or what Fritjof Capra called the 'systems view of life.'

—See Fritjof Capra, The Web of Life (1996/1997), The Hidden Connections (2002) and The Systems View of Life (2014).

Policy making should be focused on the following principles, that I may first state in simple language, then in legal language:

—A child that got lost to their parents in a crowd will in most cases be taken back to his or her family without being hurt;

—A person who is endangered to die in flames or drowned, will most probably be rescued if there are any other humans around;

—A street peddler sleeping outside in a freezing-cold winter night will most probably be rescued and taken to a shelter;

—Most people most likely pay back their debts and also their taxes;

—A so-called child killer has in most cases no intention to kill a child he abducts for sex; it is fear of discovery, shame and bewilderment that induces the impulse to kill; in other words, this impulse in not naturally there in humans, nor in humans who are sexually attracted to children; the impulse is the result of a temporary psychosis that results from the fact that relationships of this kind are uncoded by society and therefore surrounded by strong fear, shame and other negative emotions;

—A small helpless child hit by a bomb split may be saved in a war by a member of the army responsible for the bombing; simply because the man was close to that child in that moment and saw the tragedy, following his heart instead of following his orders;

—There are many examples reported from the sinking of the *Titanic* and other liners, where adults wanted to save children from drowning and thereby drowned themselves;

—In the 911 incident a number of fire police were killed because they attempted to rescue or effectively rescued men, women and children they saw in the flames.

Proposal 2/12

Legal and social policies should take into account the 'possible' human, not the 'impossible' human.

This means in practice that social policies should be based upon the assumption that humans naturally do what is good for self, others and the community and naturally avoid what is harmful for self, others and the community.

This simple reorientation at the root level of policy making would *make for much change;* it would namely minimize laws and social policies that are based on a paranoid understanding of the human nature, that is, one that is pervaded by fear and mistrust in the natural goodness of human beings.

Suspicion is not a guideline for drafting good policies. Natural life experience shows that when we give trust to others, we are trusted in return. Many corporate leaders know this and apply it in their daily management policy. Governments who trust their citizens are more trusted by them than governments that are suspicious that the citizen may want to 'break the rules.' When citizens feel they are trusted, they become more trustworthy, it is as simple as that!

—See, for example, Jean Houston, The Possible Human (1982), Michael Murphy, The Future of the Body (1992), Robert E. Ornstein, The Psychology of Consciousness (1972), Abraham Maslow, The Farther Reaches of Human Nature (1971), Part V: Society, Ervin Laszlo, Quantum Shift to the Global Brain (2008) and Noam Chomsky, Manufacturing Consent (2002).

Hence, laws should be drafted in alignment with 'positive' policy making, and in the conviction that what is preventing harm is the right policy, not the law. The law should be the *ultima ratio*, it should in the ideal case not be broken by anybody. To get there, the stress is to be put not on lawmaking, as it is now, but on the right kind of policymaking. Needless to add that it's much easier to throw a hundred new laws over the head of the citizen with every year to come than to subtly influence and change the social field in order to trigger positive law-abiding behaviors.

In natural systems all nested networks are mutually entangled, and they are co-evolving. Every single change in the system always comes about from a point of view of 'total information,' that is, the knowledge what is positively stimulating the system for growth and expansion. As a result, any little incremental change within the system is a totally informed one and will lead to growth and expansion

of the system, that is, for its overall welfare. The relationships between human beings are no different from these natural biological processes to be observed in living systems. They naturally are positive and constructive not only for self but also for others and the community at large. If humans have lost this natural 'goodness,' there are precise reasons why this happened. These reasons have been investigated by sociological and anthropological research. They are variations of one single theme, and that theme is conditioning. The strongest conditioning factors are cultural norms and laws, and social policies.

03/12

Fostering Public Sanity

Public Sanity is Public Mental Hygiene.
Republic Insanity is Absence of Governmental Hygiene.

In a world where not only particles on a quantum level, not only minds, but also countries and economies are *entangled*, nations cannot behave like in the past without triggering unpredictable chain reactions.

—See for example Amit Goswami, The Self-Aware Universe: How Consciousness Creates the Material World (1995), Dean Radin, Entangled Minds: Extrasensory Experiences in a Quantum Reality (2006), Ervin Laszlo

The global landscape has fundamentally changed over the last decades in that the original hierarchical structure has been *largely replaced* by a network structure, with the result that nations have become interdependent.

While there is still a sort of hierarchy in the sense that a minority of nations is incomparably richer than the majority, thereby having more economic thrust

power, this economic argument is not forcibly valid for the political arena.

Through international conventions, nations today are bound to behave in a manner that fosters *bilateral and multilateral cooperation and exchange.* This means that in the normal case, there is an equality of nations that more and more develops into the rule, while in the past it was the exception.

In such a situation, when a country mobilizes exorbitant resources for national defense, such doing is per se alien to the idea of international peaceful cooperation.

The military budget of the United States of America is twice the amount than the cumulated military budgets of Russia, China, Europe, and the rest of the world. That means that one nation among two hundred maintains a defense system that is *more than two hundred times tougher* and more expensive than the others.

This situation is obviously not balanced. In addition, let me repeat an old truth. Psychology teaches that safety is not guaranteed with such kind of behavior, even if the defense system is the toughest in the world.

It is much more psychologically sane and effective to have the nation contribute to the welfare and prosperity of all other nations, *thereby securing their friendly attitude and peaceful exchange,* which then can be built upon within a soundly adjusted concept of global diplomacy. Every leader knows that only those who walk their talk are followed, not those who talk their walk, and then don't walk. Grandiose promises are not what usually is the recipe for good leadership, nor is *megalomanic propaganda and complacent self-lauding.*

It is in the well-understood best of a leader nation to fight for their 'vital national interests,' but the question is how this is done, and what the strategies are for such a nation to be respected and acclaimed as a leader.

It seems that there is no fundamental difference between personal leadership, on one hand, and group or national leadership, on the other.

What leaders and leading nation states have in common is that they care for the best of the whole, not just their own best, and are predictable as to their leadership strategies. That means that those strategies have to be constantly fine-tuned in order to be well

adjusted to the political, social and economic realities. Predictability builds trust and trust is needed for leading others; a leader who is not trusted will not be able to be effective in his task to mold a certain pattern for positive behavior and attitude. To repeat it, individuals and nations are not different psychologically; they follow their trust; when they are not able to build trust they are reticent to follow the leader.

Some critics have voiced disagreement about how the United States are behaving in the world, in their role as a leader nation. Some others say the very idea of leading is wrong as well, and that in a situation of equality, no nation state can claim to be a leader.

I would think that the second alternative should not be ruled out completely, while international law develops toward more equality among nation states today, contrary to the situation still in the 19th century. As a matter of fact, it is natural that a very strong, powerful and rich nation assumes a leadership rule. It do not think there is evil in such a proposition.

However, in the analysis of a respected scholars like Noam Chomsky, there is a noted discrepancy between the moral claims the United States sets in the

world as a guideline of behavior and how the nation itself behaves on the international stage. A nation who feels responsible for the wellbeing of the globe will lead by example, and implement sustainable technologies for the sake of securing the long-term survival of all species, including the human race.

Such a nation will not only talk about peace and prosperity but practice it by implementing social and legal policies that foster inner and outer peace and friendly relationships among nations.

Such a nation will also invest all that is necessary for getting away from outdated fossil-fuel technologies, and build new ecologically sustainable technologies, be they solar, wind-driven or based upon alternative scientific concepts. As much time is needed for testing the new strategies and for implementing and realizing them commercially, the nation will carry out this important change in a timely fashion.

The most important for long-term political success and the collaboration of all people and organizations involved in the economy is *that the government 'walks its talk'*; such display of integrity then creates the momentum that is most needed in politics, namely in

form of predictability, which is based upon foresight, intelligent and effective planning.

Unfortunately, the *'hero cult'* that pervades American media culture has put all social and cultural values upside down. The hero image depicted by international media and the video game industry is about *the total opposite of the original hero archetype* known from mythology, fairy tales and folk wisdom. Instead of being a culture-founder, this false or *Oedipal Hero*, of modern vintage, is a culture-destroyer.

One may ask, perhaps naively, why a culture chooses a killer character, persecutor and spy as the model brand for its main bulk of males?

It is notorious that because of America's peculiar history, the cultural model of the male is more the outdoor kind of guy, not the homely partner type like in Europe. This being said, it is amazing to see to what extent that original mold for the male role model has been *preserved over time,* despite the structural changes from an agricultural to a postmodern industrial culture. Much speaks for the idea that it is the endlessly repeated stereotype of the male 'action guy' in cinema and television that has

contributed to stiffen and uphold the image of the white male abuser who cares about all but his partner and children, and who is rough, smelly and intellectually mediocre.

One may ask if a society can be said to be sanely adjusted that choses an abuser type as the cultural blueprint for husbands and fathers? No other culture has done that in human history, except the most violent of all there was, the tribes of Hammurabi who virtually, as it is reported in the Bible, smashed the children of their enemies 'to the ground and against walls.'

It is unparalleled in the whole of human history. And yet modern American culture can be said to be steeped, with the setup of its senseless draconian laws and the abysmal violence of its law enforcement system, in Hammurabi's infamous cultural model.

Here, an introspection about the qualities of true heroes would be an educational must, and should be written into the curricula of all educational institutions, in America and those nations that more or less imitate the American societal model. Mythology and psychology coincide to depict the true characteristics of those we call heroes. However, true

heroes realize, with commitment and consistency, but without violence, their soul values on the earth plane, thereby showing that the human potential is infinite and unlimited. We have to see that all violence is weakness, a response that shows the person's basic immaturity for facing the complexity of life and their own inner life.

Hence, the terminator kind of guy, the ruthless killer, be he a killer in the name of the so-called 'good,' is in last resort *an adolescent in revolt* who has not made the transition to true adulthood. He or she is always a false hero!

This puer mentality then, that Thomas Moore well observes and analyses in his brilliant book *Care of the Soul (1994)*, is what may be called *cultural narcissism,* and here the United States really excel in playing the main role on the stage of international relations; in fact, the nation plays the role of the revolted and repressed puer spirit that needs to 'throw a crisis' from time to time, to show that he exists and to make sure he is taken serious.

There is perhaps a time for change in so far as the adolescent nation may have grown up in the meantime, and as a result may want to have better

relationships in the sandbox of international affairs, without needing to throw sand in the eyes of another adolescent nation.

If that is the case, it is time to change the hero paradigm by changing the character of the hero image as the cultural model for males.

The consequences would be *entirely beneficial,* and they would be seen in decreasing violence, decreasing marriage disasters, and decreasing child abuse.

Proposal 3/12

An equitable state budget needs to be justified to be supported by all members of the community. It cannot be just random to fulfill this purpose.

It cannot be just arbitrary. Just because the military is a strong power factor, and a strong economic factor, a government doesn't need to run an exorbitant military budget.

The so-called 'national defense' is a term without meaning. There is nothing to defend when a nation is doing the right thing, that is, playing its positive role, instead of being a ruthless exterminator in the world.

Positive karma is created automatically by good actions. However, when a nation over the barely more than two centuries of its existence has but aggressed, bombed, murdered and genocided millions of people both on its own territory and worldwide, it has surely created bad karma! Should it then arm itself until it virtually suffocates in all its accumulated weapons?

By no means. The solution is to seek *non-coercive agreement and smooth diplomatic exchanges* with most of the other nations; the solution is to give up fictitious concepts and paranoid ideas, which are based upon

fear and that stand in the way to true and equitable relations with other nations.

An equitable budget also means to review the current situation where the education budget is about 1/10 of the military budget. Even if both budgets would be 50/50, the situation would still not be equitable. If the military budget was about 1/10 of the educational budget, I would indeed talk about equity, simply because education is more important than weapons.

The best defense in any situation of danger is a smart population, not a blown-up military apparatus!

The mercantile cause of *international child protection* needs to be replaced by real child protection which is done through a policy of empowerment, permissiveness and information.

It is done through decriminalizing all sexual behavior and educating children truthfully, by helping them build autonomy, by respecting their privacy, and intimacy, and by not manipulating them emotionally and cripple them sexually through the child sex taboo, as it is the case today. That child is the most protected that is most empowered and informed about their body and sexual function, not the child

that is kept ignorant and blindly obedient to their monolithic parents as the pillars of morality. That child is the most protected that has the authority to be himself or herself, and express their full potential both verbally and nonverbally, and that is allowed to engage in love relations of their own choice—whatever the age of the partners, provided they are not the parents of the child.

This policy entails *decriminalizing nonviolent sexual behavior* and educating children in a way that fosters autonomy, respect for their privacy, respect for their subjective intimate world, whatever this might happen to be, and last not least, refraining from brainwashing them with sexual taboos.

A state who is interested in bringing about possible humans cannot tolerate a game and television industry that perverts the masses with productions that are *overall perverse, cynical, violent and abysmally ignorant* about the real values that life fosters. Such a state, and their governments and senators will first of all define what the hero person looks like, or should look like—and when I use the term 'hero' I do this only because it's now fashionable. It may translate as 'the ideal citizen' or 'the citizen we most wish to exist' or 'the ultimately

responsible, constructive and proactive citizen.' It is thus in this sense that I use the term 'hero' here. But how is this term now defined? What we have are serial killers, terminators, and perverse, cynical, and hyper-violent machos who do their sordid business in our media world, and who ejaculate their poison in the vulnerable belly of an open society. Is this really a model for our children?

How can we tolerate this as a community, and in a democracy that understands itself as a model for all possible democracies?

Taken seriously, my argument may shatter one's ideas, while I admit that a change here is not easy to bring about.

Why? Because huge industries are involved that cannot be changed in one day. By prohibitions and a moralizing approach, nothing can be reached for the result will be revolt, especially by young people. This then could have negative repercussions in schools and colleges.

I see a change here only long-term and in case the government assigns an expert group with the task of redefining the values of male and female citizens as they are 'desirable,' based upon a study of the

behavior of all living systems. In living systems there are no 'judges', there are no 'vigilante' elements, there are no 'terminators,' there are no 'killers' for justice; the very fact of judging shows that a human being has understood nothing about true humanity. It shows only that a person uses only about 1/10 of their brain and 9/10 of their muscles, while with sane humans, it is pretty much the other way around.

To repeat it, to become judgmental here as a government, and proceed to content censorship and prohibition is not effective, and besides, it is counterproductive.

For sure, policy changes of that grandeur cannot be thrown over the head of the citizen, nor the head of corporations. So doing will only create the impression that the government is 'freedom-hostile.'

The way to go is much more subtle and complex. It is through *changing our primary school education;* it means that the values we foster for children to adopt in our *day care centers, pre-schools and primary schools* need to be double-checked, to begin with.

After checking what's actually going on here (the result may be shocking for every senator who is really open-minded to see the truth!), we need to think deep

and long for changing the structure of primary education so as to implement the values we really foster, and that are operational and constructive for the cooperative, networked, nonviolent society we want to build.

04/12

Respecting Natural Intimacy

Natural Intimacy is Conducive to Peace.
Governmental Intimidation is Conducive to Civil War.

Intimacy, *an outflow of the right of self-determination,* both within and outside the family, enjoys constitutional protection.

All sensual and sexual behavior is natural and has to be removed from the criminal code, as a matter of cultural and human sanity. Our sex laws are insane, they are legally codified 'sins,' religious prohibitions, at best, but not to be taken as serious and rational lawmaking in a modern democracy. Sorry, it is not the police's business to look and smell what humans, big or small, do under their bedcovers! What people do with their bodies is their own intimate business, not a concern for the state.

The only exception from this rule is where people do harm to each other, that is, in case they are violent, using brute force, or threat to life or torture to attain sexual fulfillment at the detriment of the partner. For

these cases, criminal laws may remain in place, but not for nonviolent sensual and sexual behavior. After all, sexual interaction is human interaction, a form of nonverbal communication that involves the body; all sexual behavior is social behavior in the sense that sexual interaction is a form of social interaction, when it is within the social code. By default, all nonviolent sexual interaction is within the social code and socially accepted, and acceptable.

Presently still controversial and not socially coded are adult-child sexual interactions, both within and without the family. While there is a rationale why parent-child sexual interaction should be restricted, there is none regarding adult-child sexual relations outside of the family web.

In the contrary was it shown in alternative child rearing experiments and the open family of the 1960s and 70s that children develop amazing social skills when they are allowed to be sexual with partners they choose, be those partners their peers or adults other than their parents.

—See, for example, Larry L. Constantin & Floyd M. Martinson (Eds.), Children & Sex: New Findings, New Perspectives (1981), Larry L. Constantine, Treasures of the Islands: Children in Alternative Lifestyles (1976) and Where are the Kids, in: Libby & Whitehurst (Eds.), Marriage and Alternatives (1977), as well as Open Family: A Lifestyle for Kids

and Other People, 26 Family Coordinator 113–130 (1977). See also Chelsea Cain & Moon Unit Zappa, Wild Child (1999), Richard Farson, Birthrights: A Bill of Rights for Children (1974) and Stevi Jackson, Childhood and Sexuality (1982).

It has been noted as well that some children prefer adults over peers. Giving children the right for free choice relations of course logically implies to let them choose the partners they like, be it adults.

—See, for example, Lauretta Bender & Abram Blau, The Reaction of Children to Sexual Relations with Adults, American J. Orthopsychiatry 7 (1937), 500–518.

When a child chooses an adult partner as his or her love and sex mate, this is not a case of pedophilia, and it is not a *'normalization of pedophilia'* in the sense of recognizing the pedophile movement's claim for political recognition. It is instead a child-focused form of permissiveness, that doesn't grant extra rights for the adults who are chosen by children or adolescents as their love mates.

However, for this to happen, the social code must be extended to encompass these relations, to give them social acceptance and latitude; to repeat it, this does not imply that the lawmaker needs to give any rights to pedophiles or those who claim political recognition of the pedophile cause.

This is an important distinction to be made, which unfortunately is *completely blurred* in the present media discussion on the subject of child rights.

It has to be seen that the family and family life are protected by the United States Constitution.

Intimacy as an *intrinsically human behavior* is protected by the family, and while it is tabooed inside of the family, it is well a subject of protection outside of the family. Intimacy is protected because without protecting intimacy, privacy could not be covered by constitutional rights. Privacy and intimacy are entangled, they go together. In all matters of intimacy, there is a concern for privacy; the same is not true the other way around, as there is well concern for privacy, for example in business transactions, where there is no intimacy involved.

Hence privacy is the overarching notion and needs stronger protection. However, in the last two decades with the rise of the 'child abuse obsession,' intimate exchange between a trusted professional (doctor or lawyer) and their client, also known as privileged communication, has since been undermined by criminal jurisprudence.

As mandated by law, clinicians (psychologists or the like), in particular, are legally obliged to disclose potential child abuse to law enforcement whenever they detect it. The client maybe warned ahead of time by the clinician during the initial interview, that any disclosure of child abuse will inevitably result in report to the police. Unfortunately, this also includes consenting or otherwise nonviolent sexual interaction. This is why a new social paradigm in needed in order to put an end to the criminalization of nonviolent or otherwise loving sexual interaction between children and adults.

If for example a hypnosis treatment reveals that the patient was having sex with underage girls or boys *at any time in the past,* the psychiatrist is deemed to report the case to law enforcement. It should be noted that the defense attorney does not share this burden that the clinician carries on his back thereby making legal counsel the supreme trusted professionals for which the notion of privileged communication still is fully honored.

It goes without saying that it is a violation of constitutional rights to strip the mental health profession of their age-old professional secret, just for complying with the exorbitant needs of specialized

police departments for closing cases 'successfully' or generally, having more cases every year, to prove their right of existence and attract more governmental attention and funding. All systems are self-perpetuating, which doesn't mean they are important and functional; nor does it mean they should exist.

For the reasons I pointed out above, such laws should not exist because they have no rationale for their existence, except we return to the Middle-Ages, but then our governments should cease to say we are living in a democracy. As things are presently, we are not yet living in a democracy. A nation that maintains spy laws of the kind the Church had under the times of the Inquisition is not a democratic, but a tyrannical nation. It is not a nation that really protects their citizens, but rather sacrifices them like scapegoats to a mythic concept of morality that is after all pure fiction.

Proposal 4/12

While the initial theme is recurring in this proposal, it really matters to have a closer look at what havoc our sex laws and their ruthless enforcement create in people's lives, in our families and neighborhoods, in our communities and in society at large.

Things have developed in ways that perhaps were not intended to happen that way two decades ago. We have created a *large-scale public hysteria* that can only be compared to the witchhunts under the Inquisition and the Nazi holocaust with its ruthless propaganda.

I may just cite one exemplary case, in addition to the others I cited before. A female university professor photographed her 6-year old masturbating son some years ago, and posted the photo on her website, with a funny comment. A few days later she was arrested and convicted for child pornography, child sexual abuse and incest. She really lost all, the boy was taken into custody, she was dismissed by her employer and in addition was publicly slandered and disgraced.

Is that how a 'democratic government' treats their smart people? Is that the way a democratic government protects the family, while it affirms in its

smear polemics virtually every day how much it loves and fosters the family?

I am saying this. No word is true of this polemic, it is one big hypocrite smear, for the family is exposed to all kinds of pranksters who can today get everybody jailed by *just a hearsay evidence* produced to any sheriff or police station, to get the muscled state machinery leashing out brutally on each and every individual concerned.

That is not a democracy, it is a demotyranny!

What is the solution?

There is no solution to paranoia, for it's not a problem but a sickness. Hence, the only 'solution' to paranoia is healing! And the healing must come through deep reflection about the insanity of the whole of the system!

05/12

Serving Children

From Protecting Children to Serving Children.
Free Choice Relations for Children.

Let me be clear about this: *child protection doesn't serve our children,* it serves the industry, and in this case, not only the industry at large, but the specific branch of industry that could be called the 'international child protection industry.'

Honestly, if child protection was not a business, I would not really be concerned about it. If it was just another paranoid vintage of fundamentalist Christianity, I would not even look at it as a lawyer and researcher. But it is not just that. It is so well-funded and makes such huge profits that we can expect it to become more influential upon society at large in the years to come, and on a global scale.

It certainly serves its business well. The question is, does it serve our children?

In my view, it is as abusive, as a strategy, in its life-denying influence upon children, as all the abuse

it claims to prevent. Not only that, its influence on society as a whole is negative and destructive; it has instituted a hate paradigm and works against any form of permissiveness. And third, it operates against social liberties and infringes upon constitutional rights.

When a child is taken from their family and put in state custody, this is a severe infringement not only of constitutional rights but also an act that can traumatize a child for life.

I think no further explanation is needed to make the reader understand that such a measure must be seen as an ultima ratio. It goes without saying that for such a measure to take, the *legal requirements must be fully met,* and this in turn means there must be strong evidence of abuse. That means the evidence must be primary, not prima facie. The ultimate burden is on the state to justify the action. When the burden of proof is on the state, it cannot be met by prima face evidence, and still less, by hearsay evidence.

Let me report a case here where the scenario was put on stage from the first to the last scene.

An American citizen, who was married and had a baby boy called a radio station to say he found out he

was a self-declared boylover, while he was married and had a child; that he sometimes was thinking of boys for love and sex and that he thought such feelings should be ultimately respected by society. The radio station called the police on the spot and the next day the baby was removed from the family and put in state custody.

The man, an intellectual, sued the government and won the constitutional action. The social worker who had executed the custody was put in jail, and the family received a compensation for the injury suffered.

Why did the man win the court action?

Because the child was put in custody without any evidence of abuse, upon the mere 'danger' that the father might one day, with his thoughts for boys, be abusive. In Germany, we call criminal law that punishes people for thoughts, *Gesinnungsstrafrecht*.

The term means 'thought-punishing criminal law.'

In Germany, such law, because it was practiced by the Nazis, is legally prohibited and unconstitutional. It seems that in the United States of America things are not that clear-cut, at least not when 'child abuse' is alleged.

But there is another important detail. All measures taken by the state against the citizen must be *equitable and proportional* so as to ensure they represent the least possible infringement of personal freedom and civil liberties. Equity is a general principle that reigns and rules the whole of constitutional law!

For example, when a thief is followed up by the police, upon robbing a bank, and the police can catch the man by merely running faster, or by encircling him, the police doesn't have the right to shoot the man, not even to shoot him in the leg. In such a case, the least possible infringement is to immobilize the man for arrest.

The exact same principle applies for cases of abuse when the measure the government wants to take is child custody. In the normal case, the custody must be pronounced by a judge except there is immediate danger for the child's safety. But even then, the principle of least possible infringement applies, and the child could be taken, for example, in custody for a few days, until the matter is verified by a judge. In the case I reported, no such temporary action had been taken and the matter was not submitted to a judge at all. The baby had been in custody for more than six months until the father won the constitutional suit

and the child was restituted to the family. Needless to add that the baby could possibly have been traumatized for life through the sudden and prolonged separation from the parents. The case thus exemplifies exactly what I am saying here:

—Child protection is no protection!

It is an unbelievable cynicism to talk about child protection, as a government, and then go and arrest children and *label them as sex offenders,* for having expressed their love with their bodies. It says that such a government *speaks with two tongues* and values compulsive morality more than lively healthy children!

Legally speaking, laws and customs that criminalize and incriminate children's physical love are a flagrant violation of international conventions for the rights of the child. They have to be abolished. Habeas corpus was first in history erected in the so-called Magna Carta (1215). It literally means 'you have the body' or 'you own your body.'

This principle was then set forth, in 1791, in the *Bill of Rights,* the *Ten Amendments* to the United States Constitution.

The amendments pertaining to the rights of the person are the 5th, the 6th and the 8th amendments. It could be argued that registering children on sex offender registries is an 'unusual punishment' mentioned in the 8th Amendment and therefore unconstitutional.

A behavior is socially adequate if a parent doing it would behave in a socially acceptable manner. For example, when a man is naked on a bed with a naked child, caressing her body, kissing her and fondling her without being exclusively focused on the child's genitals, nor having the child touch his genitals in an exclusive manner, the behavior is socially adequate because a parent doing this would act in a socially acceptable manner.

Such behavior simply is of a caring and caretaking nature, and this is today more acknowledged as ever before since we know that the strength of the child's immune system *depends on abundant tactile stimulation* in the form of stroking, caressing, kissing, licking and massaging the skin of the naked infant or child.

To construe criminal acts from physically caring behavior, be it between parents and children, be it

between adults and children outside of the family, is an alarm signal for legislative perversion.

Hence, physically caring behavior bestowed upon children of any age, and adolescents that is not targeting on *exclusive sexual gratification* should be entirely removed from the criminal code.

Proposal 5/12

Serving children implies the setup of preventive social policies, that is, policies that target at improving children's welfare, children's rights, and children's career opportunities.

The basic requirement here, before any such endeavor can bring fruit, is to substantially raise educational budgets, for all educational cycles, both on the federal and the state level.

I would argue that the most important area of child education is the nursery and pre-school level as psychoanalysis and neurology tell us that a human brain's neuronet is basically setup at the age of 6.

While it is possible to change neuronal structures by changing behavior later on in life, it is much more difficult. This means in practice that what a child can learn with relative ease, and in a playful manner, the later adult will learn only with much more effort, and through the input of relatively more time.

Let me go from the most urgent to the lesser urgent agenda points. The most urgent agenda point in improving children's welfare is to draft valid, proven and functional measures to dramatically decrease violence against children, in any form it

takes, which means to *prevent emotional abuse, physical abuse and sexual abuse.* To focus on one kind of abuse and belittle the others would be a myopic approach. To repeat it, this is not done with ever more toughening criminal laws, as criminology research clearly shows that this kind of policy leads only to more brutality in those crimes, but not to a reduction of crime.

A reduction of the incidence of abuse can only be brought about through social policies that imply the family network, the community and the collaboration between parents and teachers. It also implies that the vocational training for child nurses and teachers contains a program that brings techniques to teachers that foster emotional awareness.

Let me explain. As in real estate the motto is 'location, location, location,' in education the motto is 'relation, relation, relation.'

This is by no means a new idea or concept.

However, the United States has until recently practiced a flop-sided approach that was boosting the child's intellect while more or less neglecting to care for the child's healthy emotional growth. By contrast, more traditional educational concepts always stressed

the 'relational' aspect in education. This can be traced back to the 17th century. To mention here are two important philosophers who have written substantially about education, John Locke and Jean-Jacques Rousseau.

—See John Locke, Some Thoughts Concerning Education (1690) and Jean-Jacques Rousseau, Émile ou de l'Éducation (1762).

It is proven through research on emotional intelligence that relationship has an immediate impact on emotional intelligence.

Relationship is a quintessential life function, to be found in all living systems.

—See Fritjof Capra, The Web of Life (1996), The Hidden Connections (2002) and The Systems View of Life (2014).

Where relationships are good and non-abusive, people are thriving!

Children need to *relate to their educators* more than to their peers. This is important to understand. A peer cannot give them the emotional backup, the warmth and the feeling of welcome and protection that a good teacher can bestow. It is for that reason so important that teachers learn to be non-abusive in every respect, for which reason I have proposed a vocational training for teachers that raises awareness of possible

repressed desires that may disturb the relationship with the children in their care.

Relationship is something that needs to be learnt or re-learnt. It namely needs to be re-learnt when a person has experienced an abusive childhood background. This re-learning process is very important and may take from several months to several years. It is important because the old patterns that were wrong need to be replaced by new relational patterns and ways of how to engage and maintain relationships. This process may require psychotherapeutic help and support.

Also for children, the right way of relating to their teachers can be difficult, namely when they are either autistic or disturbed. Children from abusive homes often show fractured relationship patterns in that they tend to hijack the relationship with a teacher in a way to exclude other children, and to become 'clinging' in order to compensate for their inner void and feelings of inadequacy. This often presents a challenge to the teacher and in many cases teachers are actually overwhelmed by these children and unconsciously bestow more affection upon them than they bestow upon the normal children. This in turn is detrimental for their relationships with the larger group of normal

children and can thereby lead to fractured group communication. In these cases as well, support is needed as teachers normally do not dispose of the psychological training to handle these situations. This may be either vocational support, that is, training that is deliberately preventive for handling those constellations, or training that is given to teachers ad-hoc, by a psychologist or child psychologist.

To summarize, the relationship aspect cannot be cut away from the educational relationship without fracturing that relationship in its very essence. This is a truth that needs to be thoroughly understood by educational policy makers; it needs to be a part of the general educational approach of a nation today.

Without the relational aspect, education will inevitably bring about *narcissistic personalities,* people who are emotionally withdrawn and who are at pains with relationships as their relational skills are poor. However, especially today in our networked societies we need socially highly skilled people, which means that they should be as much as possible emotionally mature and autonomous, and unafraid of social contacts and group interaction. The next point in my educational agenda is to move from child protection to serving children. This is best done through a

redefinition of social relations that grants more autonomy to the child, and from early age. It should not be left to parents to define what autonomy means.

Autonomy proves to be a *fundamental factor* in the process of personal growth and astonishingly, tribal cultures around the world show that it is well possible to grant children a much greater sphere of autonomy as this is the case in our civilized world.

But children who are tethered to home and family lack the social skills to really move around with ease when they have grown up. They have to learn these skills in childhood, not later on when they are grown up. Relational patterns namely are laid down in the neuronet of our brain, for they belong to the fundamental 'preferred pathways' that neurology has discovered since a few decades.

Hence, governments have a substantial interest in defining, through appropriate social and educational policies, what autonomy means in the growth process for children and adolescents. This is so because more our youth develops social skills, the less they will be later dependent on the state and the more they will have the necessary skills to survive on their own and

build their social and business relations with ease and competence.

It is at this point where sexual education comes in which should not be explicit but so to speak underlying, as a non-interference pattern. In the framework of permissive education, this has been thought through already since decades but the concept was turned into oblivion through the upcoming of *tougher educational concepts* that put the stress upon protection and family enclosure.

In my view, these newer concepts are myopic in that they overlook the importance of freedom in all human growth. Children are not different from adults in that they grow better in freedom than in a corset of 'moral' duties and prohibitions that curtail down their emotional life.

Children need emotional and sexual freedom and this doesn't mean they will behave in tactless or obscene ways. It is often not understood that freedom brings about responsibility, not chaos. When it brings chaos, it was a misunderstood notion of freedom. Real freedom brings responsibility and accountability. This is valid for children just as much as for adults. But of course, it needs political courage in our days to push

such an agenda through parliament and to convince educational authorities to apply the concepts that are based on *correct research and rational policy making* than to stay with old-fashioned moralistic ideas which bring about the 'good boys' and 'good girls' that today do not fit any more in an open society that is basically freedom loving and violence-hostile.

06/12

More Public Education

More Public Education Makes for Less Crime.
More Prison Miles Make for More Crime.

The United States government *increased* the budget
for the whole of law enforcement in 2009, and
projected $26.5 billion for 2010.

The enacted Justice budget for 2008 was $22.7
billion. The Defense budget was $481.4 billion in 2008,
a 62-percent increase over 2001. Additionally, $141.7
billion were allocated for fighting 'the Global War on
Terror.' Together this is more than half a trillion
dollars spent for defense purposes only. The budget
on Education for 2008 was enacted as $57.2 billion,
which is about than one tenth of the military budget.

It is notorious that the North American Natives
and other tribal peoples do not know draconian
punishments and believe in natural justice, which is
the spiritual law of karma, the universal law of cause
and effect. As a result, they do not imprison people, or

if they do, they do it only for deliberate murder and the fine is one day, twenty-four hours, not more.

This idea is correct; nobody can think more in twenty-four years than they can think in twenty-four hours. The natives know that depriving a person from social life and natural relations with others, which include sexual relations, is the worst punishment there is. And they also know that the loss is not only on the side of the person herself, but also on the side of the community.

Our societies lose out on a *gigantic amount of human resources* because many highly intelligent and potentially creative people sit for years and decades in prisons and jails and are deprived of the basic opportunity for unfolding their intrinsic gifts and talents; had these persons remained in freedom, their personal unfoldment and creativity would have substantially enriched society at large, that is, the cultural soil of the whole metagroup.

Discarding people out from the social group is not an intelligent, nor a human practice. It is really madness, a totally destructive social policy!

When I say this I do not even talk about the huge amount of money wasted for criminal justice every

year, which could be used to substantially stock up the educational budget.

It is a destructive paradigm for human creativity and for humanity in any given society. And the worst is of course to imprison people for love, for love and sex relations, however these relations are to be named and qualified; to imprison people for love is a cultural and legal perversion!

The modern state's argument for law enforcement in the form of deprivation of freedom to be a 'human' measure compared to what was practiced in former centuries is pure cynicism. And it is simply not true.

Prison fines have been raised constantly over time, and right now have reached levels that are beyond reasonableness.

Let me give an example. In my quality as a coach, I have supported, over five years, an American citizen who had sex with the two adolescent boys of his wife. The boys had been from her former marriage. This went on for several years until the woman found out about it and called the police.

The man was convicted in Virginia and received a 135 years jail sentence. He was a self-declared boylover and did not contest the allegation in court

that he had married the woman only for gaining access to the boys. His admittedly ludicrous approach to marriage was judged as a betrayal; the obvious fact that the boys agreed to the sexual relations was completely disregarded. The man was given a rape sentence instead of one for statutory rape. That was one of the reasons for the high sentence, another was the simple fact that he was a poor man and could not afford a good lawyer.

Whatever one may think about such an admittedly controversial case, to imprison a man for lifetime for love is a *legal perversion*, and a complete judicial madness altogether. The man had not been violent in any way, and the boys clearly testified as to the tenderness of the relations, including the sexual relations, over the whole of the relationship.

The death penalty is practiced by several states of the United States. From a legal policy point of view, the death penalty has since long been considered as wrong and inhuman, in that it was seen to have no potential deterrent effect over other forms of punishment.

In addition, the moral justification of such a measure is difficult as a state who kills has little or no

convincing power that killing is not right, and must be avoided. Legal policy analysis has shown over the last decades that the only thing what the death penalty produces is a *brutalization of crime,* as a psychological defense reaction.

It has clearly been shown, as I myself have studied it at law school in Germany, that the death penalty brings about more crime, and other negative side effects than no death penalty. That is why not only the nation states in Europe, but also the European Union (EU) have explicitly abolished the death penalty. No state member of the European Union may legally institute the death penalty without at once losing its membership in the Union. In addition, one of the states practicing the death penalty, Texas, has repeatedly *electrocuted to death young boys of sixteen years,* which is to be considered as a governmentally committed crime. The death penalty against children is *violating international conventions* for the right and protection of children, as well as the United States Constitution.

When a nation publicly declares it fosters peace and democracy, and wants to bring these values to the world community, it should be taken by the word. In

addition, it should be watched when it has finished preaching its gospel and acts out ...

What the nation does since 2001 is to increase the military budget and proportionally decrease the educational budget. Every child understands that raising military budgets leads to a *potentially higher incidence of war;* in fact this truth has been proven over the whole course of human history.

Military budgets are declared as defensive, not offensive, but they are offensive in every respect. What would you think if you go in a business meeting and you see that your potential business associate is wearing a weapon attached to his or her belt? Would this increase, or rather decrease, your trust in the person, and your trust in the functionality of your business association? And would you not judge such behavior as offensive?

With military budgets it's the same because the psychological effect is exactly the same.

Go and ask any small state in the world if they trust that America, maintaining the highest military budget ever reached in the course of human history is doing this only for peace purposes, for deterring others from war, and for protecting its citizens! You

will get the reply that these are nice words and phrases and that the political reality was 'unfortunately' different.

The political reality is that the United States of America have since their establishment engaged wars with other nations, all around the world, and they have done the first step to trigger those wars, as they have done it again with Iraq, just a decade ago. These wars were thus offensive attacks, and they were led with the tanks, the bombs, and soldiers that were initially financed for 'pure defense' purposes.

This little paragraph should be taken serious especially by those citizens who still think that what governments say is of importance.

As an international lawyer I say it is of no importance, because governments tend to say what brings them profit, what serves their interest. What governments really think can be seen in the way they act, and in no other way.

Proposal 6/12

I have already outlined the limits of criminal law, when it goes against nature and the human nature, by projecting assumptions which are the result of a negative and life-denying worldview.

To repeat it, from a constitutional perspective, to declare non-harmful human behavior a crime is problematic, for it is not the business of the law to restrict human behavior where it is not doing harm to anybody. A state that practices such lawmaking must be questioned as to its legitimacy, for the state acts in a democracy as a representative of the people.

However, when such representation goes virulently against the interest of the people, it must be questioned and if necessary, reformed.

In other words, a government that uses subtle or lesser subtle ways of controlling people through the threat of draconian punishment for any little behavior that is not 'mainstream' cannot be called a democratic government. It is more of a government that systematically terrorizes people and holds them under an umbrella of hot fear that leads in the long run to public insanity. A long-term project to give prisoners access to transcendental meditation has

shown surprising results. Where such has been done as for example in Switzerland, in India and in several African nations, the result was that prisoners' behavior changed positively. In Africa the results were so dramatically positive that within just a few months whole prisons were empty for the authorities assessed these prisoners after several months of meditation as 'completely different persons' and they were freed before the end of their fines, and there was *no recidivism* of any kind! These results have been published widely and are available in the public domain.

Hence, it is but a question of political will to implement strategies of smooth behavior change that are not thrown over the head of the citizen but proposed, in a human manner, and that are respectful. Jailing people for years and decades is barbarous as a behavior and when states continue behaving in such a way in our times of change, how can they expect the citizen to change?

The budget needs to be completely remodeled and priority needs to be given to education, healthcare and humane strategies for long-term changes in behavior that are beneficial to the community.

All strategies that operate on threat, fear and punishment have to be definitely abolished for if coercion is used by the government, it must not wonder why citizens then equally use coercion for achieving their goals.

It goes without saying that only a basically integer and nonviolent government can build the legitimacy to expect nonviolent behavior from their citizens. This is not the case in the present situation, as I have demonstrated, hence the need for a fundamental change in policymaking.

07/12

Free Education

Free Education Serves the Child.
Funded Disinformation Serves State Control Over the Child.

The media world is currently changing. It used to be *entirely commercial, and commercialized,* especially in the United States.

I argue that commercial media are not free media.

It's of course already better than the media in a communist or otherwise totalitarian system where the government controls the media.

It's well one step ahead to have commercial media, but another step is needed to have free media.

This step is to have free media in both senses of the word, free in the sense of freely available at no charge and free in the sense of non-biased and as much as possible objective.

Both these free media are slowly and gradually emerging on the cultural scene. Let me give an example, Wikipedia. It's freely accessible in all countries except totalitarian Banana republics such as

Myanmar or North Korea, it's free of charge, and its content is, *cum grano salis*, objective; as humans can never be totally objective, we need to honor the effort more than the result.

The effort for Wikipedia to become ever more objective is there, is visible, it is a fact. This fact needs to be seen and honored, for it's a good and new beginning. If Wikipedia was a club that defends certain interests and manipulates the information, this would be found out and certainly infringe upon the private funding received.

As for now, it can be said that this funding is generous, coming from all walks of society, which reflects a certain and constant appreciation for this endeavor. Wikipedia can be seen as the start of a new media paradigm! Much is presently emerging on this sector, it's all free, and it's more or less useful, and without grayed-out conditions attached to it.

When I say *media should be non-commercial,* I mean they should be free of commercials. Media should not be financed through commercials. Why? When it's the industry that funds the media, the media serve the needs of the industry. This, every child understands.

How the industry forges the media toward their needs is a matter a little more subtle to understand, for it certainly can't be done by brute force, or in the way Silvio Berlusconi used to call up Italian television stations, in the midst of a talk show or the news, to shout at the presenter with all his muscle power as Italy's president.

See also that Wikipedia contains much critical content. The page on the Coca Cola Company quotes the rumors and facts to what extend the soft drink may be detrimental for our health, or the health of our children. If the industry was the sole funding agent for Wikipedia, through commercials, such content would most likely have been suppressed.

Many 'free' radio stations around the world are dependent on money they get through the insertion of commercials. To speak in these cases of 'free' radios is ridiculous in view of the fact that sponsors do tend to be very sensible to the content they are funding. This means in practice that if the content goes against their commercial interests, they won't hesitate to cut down the funding.

The only way to get around this hurdle is to receive funding from all parts of society, without any specific target group, through free donations.

Proposal 7/12

What can the government do in the media world? Should the government be active at all in the media world? I know this is a sensible question.

The government should *per se not interfere in the media,* as a matter of democratic freedom, free speech, and thus, stay away as much as possible from censorship.

About that, we all agree.

But what about the commercialization of the media, what about the corporate use of the media, if not the corporate dominance in the media?

Professor Noam Chomsky showed in one of his speeches to what extent the New York Times censors information out from print, mainly because of corporate or government interests standing in the way. He reported in this movie that, for example, the genocide in Cambodia got huge coverage because if was associated with 'communism' while the genocide in East Timor (Indonesia) got as good as no coverage because it was not associated with 'communism.'

As I suggest to change the social modeling for the male in our mainstream media and video game

productions, the question here is one of policy making.

What is the way to get there for the government without censorship of the media?

I think only a change in early education can prepare the ground for a new paradigm of male self-definition to occur. Hence, the focus is to be directed on the drafting of educational curricula that foster a male role model that is a bifurcation from the patriarchal view of the male as the hunter and outdoor kind of guy, and that implements, in the education of boys values such as *acceptance, self-knowledge, positive emotionality, intuition, caring and caregiving, sensuality and humility,* and in the education of girls, values such as *self-assertion, knowledge, positive rationality, independence, critical thinking, autonomy and natural pride.*

As the young generations today are very much focused on the role models they receive through video games and similar productions, it is not by interference in this industry that the government should proceed, for this would stir revolt and bewilderment.

The change will come through a change of the 'market' once children are educated with a different set of values, a set of values namely that is not serving corporate interests but the true interest of the child to become an autonomous, self-reliant and emotionally stable person.

08/12

Politically Neutral Science

Politically Neutral Science Promotes Truth.
Politically Correct Science Promotes Ideology.

More than 70% of American scientists are funded
by the military. They are obviously not neutral.

It goes against common sense to assume that
scientists serve the pure needs of science and are
objective in their research when they are in practice
government-funded. It is a fact that more than two
thirds of all American scientists are funded by the
military. It is naive to consider in such a case the total
amount of this accumulated research, every year, as
'objective.' I would go as far as saying that in any
other country of the world, except banana republics
and undeveloped nations, research tends to be more
objective than in the enlightened nation.

Now, what I pointed out negatively, can also be
put positively. If the wrong research is funded, this is
sad enough, but it is still more devastating when the
right research is *not funded at all.*

When I say wrong or right, I mean that of course not in a moral sense, but in the sense of scientifically valid, objective and verifiable—or not.

In the eyes of politicians, however, science that is done without regard of the 'official version' of things looks nasty and queer. And yet it is this kind of science that really brings human progress. I mention only two scientists here, whose names are famous, but in the ears of many, infamous. They are *Wilhelm Reich (1897-1959)* and *Nikola Tesla (1856-1943)*.

Both were not only not funded by the system, but were met with suspicion and denial if not outright aggression. Reich died in jail for one of his scientific discoveries, not for having stolen golden spoons.

That research must obey to ethical rules and laws was not so obvious until the emergence of genetics and biotechnology. It was more obvious regarding the protection of lab animals from senseless tortures and death inflicted 'for scientific observation.' There are now countless associations for the protection of animals, targeting ultimately at the emergence of 'the vegetarian society' which is certainly a noble goal.

But it seems to me that the general quest for clear ethical rules in all scientific research is even a nobler

and more important goal, for what is presently happening in genetics is alarming.

Let me report what one of our finest ecologists and science gurus, Fritjof Capra, has to say about the subject. Capra writes in *The Turning Point (1982/1987):*

> Another fallacy of the reductionist approach in genetics is the belief that the character traits of an organism are uniquely determined by its genetic makeup. This 'genetic determinism' is a direct consequence of regarding living organisms as machines controlled by linear chains of cause and effect. It ignores the fact that the organisms are multileveled systems, the genes being imbedded in the chromosomes, the chromosomes functioning within the nuclei of their cells, the cells incorporated in the tissues, and so on. All these levels are involved in mutual interactions that influence the organism's development and result in wide variations of the 'genetic blueprint.' (Id., p. 108)

> More recently the fallacy of genetic determinism has given rise to a widely discussed theory known as sociobiology, in which all social behavior is seen as predetermined by genetic structure. Numerous critics have pointed out that this view is not only scientifically unsound but also quite dangerous. It encourages pseudoscientific justifications for racism and sexism by interpreting differences in human behavior as genetically preprogrammed and unchangeable. (Id., p. 109)

More specifically on the subject of biotechnology, genetic manipulation and the *devastating consequences* of their unethical maneuvering, Capra writes in his later book *The Hidden Connections (2002)*:

> Geneticists soon discovered that there is a huge gap between the ability to identify genes that are involved in the development of disease and the understanding of their precise function, let alone their / manipulation to obtain a desired outcome. As we now know, this gap is a direct consequence of the mismatch between the linear causal chains of genetic determination and the nonlinear epigenetic networks of biological reality. (Id., p. 178)

> The reality of genetic engineering is much more messy. At the current state of the art, geneticists cannot control what happens in the organism. They can insert a gene into the nucleus of a cell with the help of a specific gene transfer vector, but they never know whether the cell will incorporate it into its DNA, nor where the new gene will be located, nor what effects this will have on the organism. Thus, genetic engineering proceeds by trial and error in a way that is extremely wasteful. The average success rate of genetic experiments is only about 1 percent, because the living background of the host organism, which determines the outcome of the experiment, remains largely inaccessible to the engineering mentality that underlies our current biotechnologies. (Id.)

The real ethical problems surrounding the current cloning procedure are rooted in the biological developmental problems it generates. They are a consequence of the crucial fact that the manipulated cell from which the embryo grows is a hybrid of cellular components from two different animals. Its nucleus stems from one organism, while the rest of the cell, which contains the entire epigenetic network, stems from another. Because of the enormous complexity of the epigenetic network and its interactions with the genome, the two components will only very rarely be compatible. (Id., p. 183)

With the new chemicals, farming became mechanized and energy intensive, favoring large corporate farmers with sufficient capital, and forcing most of the traditional single-family farmers to abandon their land. All over the world, large numbers of people have left rural areas and joined the masses of urban unemployed as victims of the Green Revolution. (Id., p. 186)

The long-term effects of excessive chemical farming have been disastrous for the health of the soil and for human health, for our social relations, and for the entire natural environment on which our well-being and future survival depends. As the same crops were planted and fertilized synthetically year after year, the balance of the ecological processes in the soil was disrupted; the amount of organic matter diminished, and with it the soil's ability to retain moisture. The resulting changes in soil texture entailed a multitude of

interrelated harmful consequences—loss of humus, dry and sterile soil, wind and water erosion, and so on. (Id.)

The ecological imbalance caused by monocultures and excessive use of chemicals also resulted in enormous increases in pests and crop diseases, which farmers countered by spraying ever larger doses of pesticides in vicious cycles of depletion and destruction. The hazards for human health increased accordingly as more and more toxic chemicals seeped through the soil, contaminated the water table and showed up in our food. (Id., pp. 186–187)

Through a series of massive mergers and because of the tight control afforded by genetic technologies, an unprecedented concentration of ownership and control over food production is now under way. The top ten agrochemical companies control 85 percent of the global market; the top five control virtually the entire market for genetically modified (GM) seeds. Monsanto alone bought into the major seed companies in India and Brazil, in addition to buying numerous biotech companies, while DuPont bought Pioneer Hi-Bred, the world's largest seed company. The goal of these corporate giants is to create a single world agricultural system in which they would be able to control all stages of food production and manipulate both food supplies and prices. (Id., pp. 187–188)

Biotechnology proponents have argued repeatedly that GM seeds are crucial to feed the world, using the same

flawed reasoning that was advanced for decades by the proponents of the Green Revolution. Conventional food production, they maintain, will not keep pace with the world population. (Id., p. 188)

In addition, it should be considered from a policy making perspective that the principle of peer review as established all over the world, is in final account destructive for the progress of science.

I have myself not found scientific recognition because of the simple fact that my scientific papers were not subjected to peer review. This started back in the 1980s when my doctoral thesis in international law was done at the wrong university in the wrong country, and in the wrong language.

I was awarded two scholarships from Swiss universities, Lausanne and Geneva, in addition to a Fulbright Travel Grant for my postgraduate work at the University of Georgia, USA. Despite the opportunity to finalize my thesis at UGA, for ethical reasons, I returned to Switzerland as I had received funding for my research. However, as it involved an extensive review of the Anglo-American law of evidence, Swiss scholars had no idea what I was talking about in my thesis, at the law faculty of the

University of Geneva. My thesis director openly admitted he was incompetent to evaluate my thesis.

I prided myself writing the thesis in French language, which was boosting my skills of the French language, but not my academic recognition. French and Swiss scholars did not care a single bit about the importance of the burden of proof in matters of foreign sovereign immunity litigation, while many lawyers in the United States and Great Britain are specialized in this kind of affairs.

As a result, I clearly failed not because of lacking efforts, or lacking brilliance, but because of being reviewed by incompetent people. For the public presentation of my thesis, the so-called *soutenance de thèse*, Lady Fox, Q.C. was invited from London, a leading specialist on foreign sovereign immunity. Lady Fox gave me a *summa cum laude* and was angered at the fact that the other members of the jury did not follow and gave me bad notes, doing this, as she openly told me, because 'they have not understood a bit of your thesis.'

That is why I can say that the requirement of peer review is a stumble stone for many brilliant researchers who, like me, end up in oblivion because

their financial situation did not allow them to pay the tuition of a good university in a country where their work would elicit academic interest.

Unfortunately, I did not listen to advice to stay in the United States, refusing the offer of becoming professor there and publish my thesis, as I thought it was unethical to do so because I got the scholarships from Switzerland.

Destiny showed me that my ethical scruples were misplaced, as in the United States I would have got the peer review of my work that I so badly needed.

Lady Fox had asked me to come to England, but she could not offer me a scholarship or assistantship which is why, at that time, I was unable to accept her offer because of mere financial constraints.

My thesis was not printed either. Printing costs being excessively high in Switzerland, I would have had to invest thirteen thousand Swiss Francs. The university had offered me a grant of five thousand Swiss Francs but I did not have the remaining eight thousand Swiss francs for financing the printing of my thesis. Hence, to this day, my doctoral thesis, that took me five hard years to accomplish, is not printed, and not published anywhere.

Eventually, in 2010, I offered an English version of my thesis work it to *Oxford University Press (OUP)* and they refused publishing it with the most dubious reasons that one can come up with. It is really a scandal! I have however finally published it with amazon.com and feel honored and rewarded about this great opportunity. But it does not sell, and nobody gives feedback on it!

If this is not a story to consider, I don't know any that could be more convincing of the fact that the requirement of peer review is a guillotine for many brilliant researchers.

Proposal 8/12

The government should develop a functional view of science, not a view that is conditioned by the 'usefulness' of science for specific agendas, as for example national defense or child protection, feminism or homosexuality. These are all *partial interests* while the overwhelming objective of science is observation of nature and the *systematic cataloguing of data in a comprehensive system* which can be shared among scientists and the public at large because of a concise scientific terminology.

It has been assessed by erudite researchers on linguistics such as Professor Noam Chomsky that not only science, but any kind of information sharing, be it intuitive, can only proceed from a basis of shared terminology, where the term 'terminology' has to be seen in its widest sense. This is involved in all human verbal communication.

But in science, we are at a higher level still of such communication, a level namely where imprecision can be fatal to the scientific system and scientific exchange. Hence the need for a much more precise terminology than that which is used in daily life. Let me give an example.

Before our science recognized the field, zero-point field, quantum field, unified field or quantum vacuum, which was only a recent achievement, this notion was discussed as an alternative science doctrine under the most various names.

Precisely because the notion was heretic under the Church's science codex, the whole of this research had to be underground, hidden from the mainstream, and secret.

It was among the alchemists that it started, mainly with Paracelsus (1493–1541), the great natural healer.

He called this subtle energy *vis vitalis* or *mumia*.

After him, there was Emanuel Swedenborg (1688–1772), the great scholar, who discovered exactly the same and called it *spirit energy*.

The next was the German doctor Franz Anton Mesmer (1734–1815) who called the vital energy *animal magnetism* and was able to produce spontaneous healing by applying magnets, only to find out later on that the healing would occur in the same way without the magnets, as an effect of his own body.

After Mesmer, we got the German chemist and nobleman Baron Carl Ludwig Freiherr von

Reichenbach (1788–1869) who called the subtle energy *Odic Force* or simply *Od*.

The next in line within this alternative science tradition was Wilhelm Reich (1897–1957) who called this energy *orgone*. His contemporary Georges Lakhovsky (1968–1942), a Russian electric engineer found the same through experiments with cell resonance and came to call the cosmic radiation *universion*.

Finally, before the great change to quantum physics, there was Harold Saxton Burr (1989–1973) who called this subtle energy the *L-Field*. This was the first time that a scientist saw that it's actually not an energy but a field, a pattern, and that the term 'energy' was misleading because it is confounded with kinetic energy. This energy field has absolutely nothing to do with kinetic energy, or rather, kinetic energy is a result of it, as all life is a result of it. This subtle energy field is, as we know today, the creator force in the universe.

This research showed me that without a *consistent terminology* science is actually jungle science. I created that terminology while it's not the one that is now used in quantum physics. I have created it because it

integrates the old traditions while quantum physics and its new vocabulary shuns the old traditions by denying their very existence, by claiming all of this was a 'new discovery,' as Ervin Laszlo does in his book *Science and the Akashic Field (2004)* in which he mentions not with one word all of this research.

This is exactly the deplorable hubris of our modern science, which has its root in government funding and the resulting attitude of funded scientists to produce research results that are 'politically correct.'

Hence, the need for a change.

09/12

Humanism and Realism is Objective Perception.
Idealism and Ideology is Distorted Perception.

J. Krishnamurti has shown in all his talks that our culture is *pervaded with a misplaced idealism* that widely distorts our perception interface and sense of reality.

We are dividing life in what is and what should be, thereby putting up a fence between the world and our idealized version of it. This split really is pathological because it distorts our entire sense of living. It leads straight to fragmentation in that we will be divided in a realist, that is, the one who sees *what is,* and an idealist or ideologist who longs for *what should be*, 'if the world was ideal.'

Much blood has been shed for social ideas and ideals that were *antisocial* in the sense that they were bringing people up against each other.

All bloody revolutions were founded upon one or the other social ideal.

However, it is not with ideals that we can improve society, our human togetherness, and our social and legal policies. It's only possible when we make the cultural split undone and see the world as a platform of infinite possibilities, as a framework that operates on a quantum level in realms of pure potentiality.

As all creation is an inside-out movement from the quantum level to tangible reality, from the ethereal to the manifest: the realms of thought, and the invisible realms of emotion and imagination, the gift of feeling are the co-evolving elements in this creative process.

But we are shutting ourselves off from being creative when we put up ideals. To be creative means to live without any ideals, and to remain open for total perception of *what is.*

This is why change, positive change, for our society can only start from the moment we are living with *what is,* discarding all ideas of what *should be.*

This means we build vision instead of daydreaming, we build viable concepts instead of political science fiction.

Social utopias are on the same level as ideals, they are another vintage of ideals, and as such they are useless in real and tangible social policy making. They

have contributed to the split paradigm that puts up the 'negative human' as a problem to cope with, and the 'positive human' as an ideal to be longed for.

Fact is that the human is perfect, and all true religion recognizes this fact. But our religions are not natural since many hundreds of years, they are far from the truth, which is why they project on the human their negative life paradigm, coming up with the false idea that the human being is somehow corrupt, 'born in sin,' imperfect and mean, and needs to be bettered, reformed, improved and reborn as a 'spiritual being.'

All this is complete nonsense. The human being is spiritual by nature and doesn't need to be improved.

All creation is perfect; it needs no improvement. Why things went wrong over the whole course of patriarchy till today is that human beings do not consider themselves as what they are, but have collectively developed a negative life paradigm that considers the 'negative human,' the impossible human, as the social reality.

I contend that we have to focus on the positive or possible human, not the impossible or negative human which is a mere projection.

The real human is the *possible human.* Only on this basis can we eventually forge viable, sustainable social and legal paradigms that are reasonable enough for the whole of society to be accepted, respected, and followed.

What we have right now is a situation that ultimately leads to so far hidden rebellion, which can very quickly evolve into anarchy, and civil war. Our social and legal policies, in vital areas of life, regarding our pleasure function, for example, are outdated, irrational, and even insane, and what they do in the long run is to bring people up against their government, and against each other. Thus, they are socially and culturally destructive!

The mass media profit from this abysmally ludicrous and dangerous social situation, by playing on the perverse feelings of many a 'homo normalis' who needs to abreact their silent hate and inner revolt against 'the system.'

This really leads to more violence, more social dissent, more upheaval and in last resort, if nothing is done to remedy the wrong policies, to civil war.

The whole of patriarchy was not based upon a rational and sane assessment of nature, and of human

nature. It could not get there simply because it never wanted to accept nature, which means to accept the female and female values.

Hence, instead of assessing and integrating nature, it has projected intellectual assumptions upon nature, thereby distorting human perception to a degree that it resulted in an upside-down view of life, which is a process I call *cultural perversion.*

All original pre-patriarchal tribal cultures were nonjudgmental; they did not judge life. Instead, they understood the subtle logic of the universe and therefore were leading plain, whole and integral lives. As a result, they lived peacefully, and in positive communication with nature. Idealism was unknown to them.

Idealism is an intellectual construct that is a result of frustration, and disintegration from the wholeness of life, our *natural continuum,* which includes the emotional, the sexual, and the spiritual dimension. All these three dimensions were discarded out by patriarchy!

Patriarchy's morality code posited that any 'good life' is to be lived in a non-emotional, non-sexual and non-spiritual dimension. Emotionality was replaced

by fierce and arrogant intellectualism! Sexuality was replaced by compulsive child-breeding through raping the marriage partner, thereby *institutionalizing rape* as the single most accepted sexual act, while paying lip-service to the contrary.

And spirituality was replaced by compulsory religion in the form of worshipping a paranoid and murderous god-figure, called YAHWEH, that was a mere projection of human imperfection put on the stage of an imaginary 'eternal theater.'

So where are we now? Are we still entangled in the paranoid plot called patriarchy that is on stage since five thousand years and that preaches persecution, torture, murder and death as its prime values, or are we getting beyond this cultural madness, once for all?

Realism is a notion that was completely distorted by Cartesian science, and generally, the Cartesian reductionist worldview that discards out more from life than it admits, ending up with a residue or a torso of life—a mutilated construct that is based upon paranoia, not upon human sanity.

A realistic worldview, under the Cartesian paradigm, was a total reduction of life, to the point to

end up with a caricature of life and living. However, this is not what realism is about when resorting to the original meaning of the term. Realism means to be objective, as much as possible. Humans cannot be totally objective, they are objective and subjective at the same time. The only thing humans can do with regard to their perception of reality is to strive for objectiveness—without ever attaining it.

The false and doctrinaire view under patriarchy was that the male is by nature objective and the female by nature subjective. Needless to say that, by now, this is recognized by a majority of social and natural scientists to be a pure myth. The truth is that females tend to be more objective than males, for example in the science world.

This has been demonstrated by research over and over again. In addition, females tend to be more courageous than males to defend their objective scientific assessment when under stress or being criticized.

Females also are more redundant to react objectively when under pressure than males in the same kind of situations. Incidentally, males tend to be more violent, that is, psychologically lesser robust

than women in situations involving high psychic stress.

Hence, being realistic means to be more grounded in tangible reality than this was and is the case in cultures that are founded upon religious ideologies, such as, for example, orthodox, fundamentalist Christian or Muslim societies.

Now, from this insight, there is but a step to see it embedded in the human world, in the human sphere.

The human being, to repeat it, is gifted with both a tendency to be objective and to be subjective, to be rational and to be irrational. Both qualities are complementary in the sense that humans need both these qualities to function completely, freely and creatively.

This means in practice that when irrational reasoning and behavior is discarded out of communication, the communication process will be distorted; incidentally, this leads to the paradoxical result that when communication is forced to be rational, it will become more irrational. When we focus upon human life and society and ask what is realistic behavior, or a realistic attitude, we have to

consider the total human, that means the human who is both rational and irrational.

This will lead us quite automatically to a humanistic understanding of life and humanity, and of human behavior. This, in turn, will lead us to be more open and permissive regarding humans, and thus more human-friendly.

From this starting point, our social and legal policies will be much more adapted to the nature of humans, instead of being, as now, adapted to the nature of compulsive morality and thus to an intellectual construct that has no real existence in life. To see this means to understand that our present social policies are made for dummies, not for humans.

Proposal 9/12

All great ideals have brought about bloodshed throughout human history. Lao-tzu wrote in the *Dao De Ching* that when society falls into decay and depravation, filial love becomes important, and idealism and patriotism are in high value.

All the great war criminals during WW2 were idealists. Hitler was an idealist, Franco was an idealist, Mussolini was an idealist, Stalin was an idealist, Mao was an idealist, Pol Pot was an idealist. Yet they were all war criminals and have committed large-scale genocide. And the list goes on and on.

To bring about sanity in our society, we need to free our school curricula from idealism and have to replace it with *realism*. What does that mean in practice? Realism looks at *what-is*, idealism strives for what *should-be*. It is obvious that realism is closer to day-to-day reality and immediate perception, and idealism closer to day-dreaming and heroic fantasies that lead nowhere.

Thus the agenda here for the government is to see that schools and universities offer a practical and useful education that is as much free of religious, moral and patriotic ideals. Patriotism and nationalism

do not serve us, they lead to social and political retardation, and they defeat the social agenda. Religious values may have a place in society but they should never be used to condition and indoctrinate students. Realism leads to a pragmatic approach in education that leads to positive results and enhances effectiveness!

10/12

Promoting Pleasure as a Positive Life Function Reduces Violence.
Condemning Pleasure as Negative Morality Raises Violence.

It has been demonstrated by research over the last four decades that there is a mutually exclusive relationship between pleasure and violence.

Back in 1973, the British neurologist Herbert James Campbell published a thought-provoking book, entitled *The Pleasure Areas.* In his book Campbell retraces his own research but also the research of a number of other neurologists who came to the result to assume a mutually exclusive relationship, in our brain, between pleasure in violence.

To put it in a formula, when the brain runs on pleasure, it doesn't run on violence, and vice versa.

Locally in the brain, there are regions for pleasure and for violence. When the pleasure areas are stimulated, the violence areas are inactive, and vice versa.

This means that when a society fosters pleasure, it is little violent, and when a society such as ours says 'violence is better than sex,' it fosters violence through a marked reduction of the pleasure function. Next, the American developmental neuropsychologist James W. Prescott, Ph.D., ventured into the daringly new and controversial research on violence that is now to be considered the leading edge in neuroscience, behavioral psychology and research on positive human evolution.

I retraced Prescott's revolutionary research over a number of years, for it was never published conclusively in a properly published research volume, but is scattered all over the Internet. The truth is that Prescott never found a publisher, and that, once again, is symptomatic for our allegedly so democratic society!

When it goes to unveil the hidden connections that explain why our culture is violent, and why it spreads this violence worldwide, there are only closed doors.

Back in 2010, I had published all those findings, including the United Nations research on violence against children in one monograph, and the book, while it was first published with Createspace /

Amazon, was about one month later torn down by Amazon and blocked in my Createspace account.

No reason was given for this barbarous undemocratic censoring of valid content and all my dozens of emails remained unreplied to until this very day!

Recently, Dr. Prescott has published a DVD entitled *The Origins of Love & Violence: Sensory Deprivation and the Developing Brain,* which contains a wealth of research documentaries on the roots of violence in our culture.

I discovered the writings of James W. Prescott back in the 1980s, at a time when I was evaluating the research of Ashley Montagu, Frederick Leboyer, Michel Odent, Alexander Lowen, and Bronislaw Malinowski.

The two major articles written by James W. Prescott, that I discuss in several of my books were coming to me like a revelation to a question I had asked since more than a decade: 'What are the roots of violence?'

Knowing from anthropological studies and from spiritual work that violence is not the natural condition for humanity, but a sort of emotional and

cultural perversion that results from deep hurt suffered early in childhood, and probably also from scars that go back to former lives, I was grateful to have found at least one conclusive research that not only analyzed our condition, but also pointed to viable solutions.

The solutions that Dr. James Prescott suggests, are changes in the process of child birth and our educational system, a *permissive and nonviolent child-rearing paradigm, social permissiveness regarding premarital sex and a definite legal prohibition of physical punishment of children in both the home and school together with effective government collaboration in fighting domestic violence.*

To begin with, regarding infant care, Dr. Prescott stresses the importance of primary symbiosis between mother and infant during the first eighteen months of the infant, abundant tactile stimulation of infants and babies, using techniques of child massage, as well as co-sleeping between parents and small children. It is interesting to note that the suggestions Dr. Prescott comes up with from his perspective as a peace researcher are very much in accordance with those suggested by Jean Liedloff, in her book *The Continuum*

Concept (1977/1986), which is a vivid account of the integrated and wistful lifestyle of native peoples.

Also, there is a striking similarity of solutions offered for the same problems by Ashley Montagu, as a result of his decades of skin research, and by the French obstetricians Michel Odent and Frederick Leboyer who have looked beyond the fence of obstetrics and into what Odent called *Primal Health,* to formulate a holistic concept of health and wellbeing.

James W. Prescott has now realized together with Michael Mendizza the educational DVD for the prevention of violence and the transmission of the important research insights, for raising public awareness of the etiology of violence and the importance of paradigm changes in social sciences as well as governmental policy making.

In detail, the DVD contains over three hours of historical film footage, in-depth interviews and a comprehensive research database (1966–2008).

Twenty-five years of NICHD brain-behavior research document how *early sensory deprivation, abuse and neglect* patterns the brain for a lifetime of depression and violence. Dr. Prescott's research also found that baby-carrying during the first year of life

and breast feeding for two and a half years or longer optimizes brain-behavioral development for peaceful, harmonious and egalitarian behaviors.

Here are more research results that document the following principles, valid for all cultures:

—Pain and pleasure experienced early in life shapes the developing brain for peace or violence;

—Complex neural networks are produced by sensory stimulation; impoverished neural networks by sensory deprivation;

—These two sensory processes shape two different brains: the *neurodissociative* or *neurointegrative* brain;

—Neural networks formed early in life influence the neural networks in the later developing neocortical brain, the brain system for the formation of social and moral values of culture;

—Children reared under conditions of pleasure (affectional bonding) are placed on a life path of affection, peace, harmony and egalitarianism;

—Most children reared under conditions of suffering (affectional deprivation) are placed on a life path of depression, violence, authoritarianism and suicide;

—Violent cultures impair brain development—the *neurodissociative* brain, which prevents the development of the *neurointegrative* brain and peaceful behaviors;

—Cultures throughout the world must recognize the full equality of the feminine with the masculine, if affectionate and sexually nonviolent relationships are to prevail.

Dr. Prescott's long-term research targets at reducing violence within society, all forms of violence, that is, domestic violence, sexual violence, structural violence, and especially violence against women and children.

The failure of intimacy in the mother-infant/child relationship is the principle cause of depression and violence, which can best be prevented by breastfeeding for 'two years of age and beyond,' as recommended by WHO/UNICEF in the Innocenti Declaration of 1990; and by baby-carrying during the first year of life.

The Dalai Lama stated in *Ethics For The New Millennium (1999)*:

Despite the body of opinion suggesting that human nature is basically aggressive and competitive, my own

view is that our appreciation for affection and love is so profound that it begins even before our birth… A happy mother bears a happy child… Almost without exception, the mother's first act is to offer her baby her nourishing milk—an act which to me symbolizes unconditional love… What we see instead is a relationship based on love and mutual tenderness, which is totally spontaneous. It is not learned from others, no religion requires it, no laws impose it, no schools have taught it. It arises quite naturally.

The Dalai Lama affirms that mothers' breastfeeding is an act of 'unconditional love;' this observation is consistent with Dr. Prescott's research results reporting that 77% (20/26) of cultures with weaning age of 2.5 years or greater are rated low or absent in suicide and 82% (14/17) of these cultures which support youth sexual love are rated low or absent in suicide.

Additional studies found that 86% (31/36) of cultures with weaning age of 2.5 years or greater were rated low or absent in suicide.

Hence, compassion and unconditional love are first learned at the breast of the mother.

In recent years many new statutes and laws have been forged by our national parliaments that were put through in a hurried manner, if they were not just

legal ad-hoc replies to asocial or criminal cases and events, such as the so-called 'Megan Laws.' Such kind of lawmaking tends to be both remiss in attention to long-term legal policy and irrational or even excessive in 'punishing' socially undesired behavior.

Only *long-term legal policy* effectively prevents violent asocial behaviors. Ad-hoc laws, however, contribute to the feeling that they are somehow arbitrary, undemocratic, tyrannical, unjust and excessive.

In addition, it's a fact that humans tend to disregard laws that they perceive as unreasonable or 'impossible to follow' in their outreach.

Hence, to draft excessive laws without inserting them into long-term legal and social policy making means down the road to draft ineffective laws.

This is why the situation regarding violence and abuse in our society, as the media repeat saying, gets worse and worse. The culprit here is first of all wrong lawmaking, and *negligent long-term social policy making*.

It must be seen that it's relatively easy to throw new laws over the head of the citizen, and that it is more time-consuming and thought-provoking to

insert a number of laws consistently into a long-term strategy of comprehensive and socially acceptable policy making. This namely requires governments to think long and deep about the problems that their laws tackle; and often it will be seen that the right approach of dealing with social problems is not to draft laws, but to care for preventing socially undesired behavior, as a measure or measures on the purely social level!

Prevention needs intelligent and diligent research, it needs governments to *collaborate* with scientists, universities, and the media, it needs attention to detail, and understanding of human complexity.

When governments fail to *responsibilize* themselves for really tackling the social issues at stake today, they are proving to be sloppy in their overall approach to ruling the community; then, they have to be replaced.

Hurried lawmaking is irresponsible governmental behavior; the only things that such lawmaking produces is public hysteria, chaos, and still longer prison miles every year.

Prescott's research, besides its new insights and results, references a wealth of research that he reports and summarizes in his papers. When going through

this research, one really finds no long-standing theory that was ever proven to be true and that affirms the 'impossible' human as the standard human prototype. Much to the contrary will one recognize that humans can be conditioned in all possible ways, and thus, that the human potential, so to say, is open for every possible existential framework.

It's precisely the lack of instincts, such as they are found with mammals, that makes the human being so complex, but also so endangered when it comes to violence as a totally conditioned response, a response that originally is not contained in the human setup.

Hence, when we see that violence is a conditioned response, we have to think deep and hard what those conditions are that produce violence. The answers we get are precise, and to the point. We know the conditions, one by one, we know what are the social or rather unsocial circumstances that condition humans for violence. These circumstances, when they form the basic ingredients of a culture, then produce what I call a 'wrong culture' or a 'perverse culture' or else an 'upside-down culture.'

For example, research on the roots of violence clearly affirms that when infants are raised in a

climate of sensory deprivation, when premarital sex is prohibited, when females and female children are socially devalued, to state only these three factors among a variety of others, there is a 100% prediction that this particular mix will produce violent humans for the next generation.

When these patterns are cultural patterns in the sense that a majority of humans behave in that unnatural and deprivatory manner, then there is again a 100% prediction that that culture is violent.

Thus, to summarize, there is no wishy-washy position possible regarding these fundamental research insights, as the results are clear-cut!

James W. Prescott formulated the essence of his research in a social policy strategy entitled *Ten Principles of Mother-Infant Bonding:*

"1—Every Pregnancy is a Wanted Pregnancy. Every Child is a Wanted Child. Unwanted children are typically unloved, abused and neglected who become the next generation of delinquents, violent offenders and alcohol/drug abusers and addicts.

2—Every Pregnancy Has Proper Nutrition & Prenatal Care—medical and psychological—and is free from

alcohol, drugs tobacco and other harmful agents of stress.

3 — *Natural Birthing* — avoid wherever possible obstetrical medications, forceps & induced labor with no episiotomy nor premature cutting of umbilical cord.

4 — *Mother controls the birthing position* with no separation of newborn from mother. Newborn maintains intimate body contact with mother for breastfeeding and nurturance that promotes basic trust.

5 — *No Circumcision of the Newborn.* The traumatic pain of newborn circumcision adversely affects normal brain development, impairs affectional bonding with mother and has long lasting effects upon how pain and pleasure are experienced in life that shapes the development of human trust.

6 — *Breastfeeding On Demand* by the newborn/infant/child and for 'two years or beyond,' as recommended by the World Health Organization (WHO) and UNICEF. Failure to breastfeed results in positive harm to normal brain development and to the immunological health of the newborn, infant and child. Encoding the developing brain with the smell

of the mother's body through breastfeeding is essential for the later development of intimate sexuality.

7—*Intimate Body Contact* is maintained between mother and newborn/infant by being carried continuously on the body of the mother for the first year of life. Such continuous gentle body movement stimulation of the newborn/infant promotes optimal brain development and 'Basic Trust' for peaceful/happy behaviors. Mother-infant co-sleeping is encouraged for 'two years or beyond.' Mother-infant/child body contact can also be optimized with daily infant/child massage. Father must also learn to affectionately bond with his infant by being an additional source of physical affection and supporting mother as a nurturing mother.

8—*Immediate Comforting* is given to infants and children who are crying. No infant/child should ever be permitted to cry itself to sleep, which impairs development of Human Trust.

9—*Infants and Children are for hugging* and should never be physically hit for any reason. Merging childhood parental love with parental violent pain helps create adult violent 'love.'

10—Infants and Children are honored and should never be humiliated nor emotionally abused for any reason. The emerging sexuality of every child is respected which promotes Human Trust. Mothers must be honored and not replaced by institutional day care which emotionally harms children before three years of age. Mother-Infant/Child community development centers must replace institutionalized day care."

Dr. Prescott stresses that the most critical early life experiences are formed in the mother-infant relationship, and that this early conditioning affects all our later relationships and the development of culture.

Prescott's research demonstrates the role of body pleasure in affectional bonding in the mother-infant relationship and in the human sexual relationship as an important factor in the formation of nonviolence in the individual and in human cultures. In his article *Prevention or Therapy or the Politics of Trust (2005)*, Dr. Prescott shows that basic trust must occur before a politics of trust can be formed to effect changes at the individual and cultural levels and to transform violent individuals and cultures into peaceful individuals and cultures.

He also explains the limitations of psychotherapy in effecting changes in the damaged emotional-social-sexual brain, as psychotherapy tends to reach only the neo-cortical brain, but not the subcortical brain.

Prescott's insights result in his astonishing statement that 'as culture shapes the developing brain, so the brain shapes culture.' He refers in his paper to *Childhood and Society (1950/1963)* by Erik H. Erikson, who was perhaps the first psychologist to assert that without the foundation of basic trust, which is formed during the early years of the life cycle, basic mistrust takes its place, which influences all future stages in the human life cycle. Erickson writes:

> It is now possible that only an equal, well-polarized maturation of all-human maternal and paternal care can save mankind . . . But this demands that a future involvement in motherhood and fatherhood must be based on the unifying polarity of a maternally shared earthly space and a paternal sense of a joint conservation and defense of such space. (Id., 10–11)

Prescott reports that depression, social alienation, impulse dyscontrol, chronic stimulus-seeking behaviors, violence against oneself (self mutilation

and suicide) and others (homicidal assaults), maternal violence and sexual dysfunctions are some of the behavioral consequences documented in animals and humans consequent to mother-infant separation.

He summarizes that high affectional bonding in the maternal-infant relationship and adolescent sexual relationships (youth sexual behavior being supported and not punished) could predict with 100% accuracy the peaceful or violent nature of 49 tribal cultures he examined, based upon Textor's cross-cultural summary.

He writes in *Prevention Or Therapy And The Politics of Trust Inspiring a New Human Agenda (2005)*:

> This 49-culture study used all the available information in the 400-culture sample of Textor (1967) where information on both baby-carrying bonding and violence ('torture, mutilation and killing of enemy captured in warfare') was available on these 49 tribal cultures. (…) The behavioral matrixes of patrilineal and matrilineal tribal cultures reveal the remarkable similarity of the patristic tribal cultures with the patristic monotheistic cultures of 'Western civilization,' which are also violent, sexually puritanical/exploitive and god centered (Prescott, 1975, 1977, 1989, 1990, 1996, 2001). (…) These findings are consonant with the observations of psychoanalyst Wilhelm Reich on the role of women and sexuality in a free and egalitarian

society when he stated: 'Sexually awakened women, affirmed and recognized as such, would mean the complete collapse of the authoritarian ideology.'

In *Affectional Bonding for the Prevention of Violent Behaviors (1990),* Dr. Prescott explains his theory comprehensively for the novice reader, and the researcher who is not yet familiar with the details of his cross-cultural and multi-disciplinary research:

> The failure to develop peaceful behaviors represents the single greatest threat to the quality of human life and to the survival of human civilization. The human mammal is unique in its ability to engage in collective action to destroy its own species. Perhaps the evolution of language and complex cognitive functioning are the indispensable factors accounting for the uniqueness of human violence. Alternately, our evolutionary heritage, wherein the most aggressive individuals survived hostile and violent environments, may have led to the development of an aggressive genotype. No such genotype has, of course, been found, and it is highly unlikely that such a genotype exists. The enormous extent and diversity of human violence throughout the world appears to defy any simple genetic explanation. Fortunately, there is another explanation. It is my belief that the origins of human violence have primarily an ontogenetic basis with unique phylogenetic characteristics, in brief, my SAD (Somatosensory Affectional Deprivation) theory states that the failure

to develop affectional bonds in human relationships is the primary cause of human violence. The beginning of this failure is in the parent-offspring relationship where sensory deprivation of the emotional affective senses (tactile, vestibular, olfactory sensory modalities) is permitted to occur. It is these sensory modalities that mediate somatosensory affectional pleasure experiences in the parent-offspring relationship, which are held to be necessary for the development of primary affectional bonds between parent and offspring. (Id., 95)

In addition to this research, Dr. Michel Odent from France has done an important contribution through his own more than twenty years of research on the human pleasure function. *The Functions of the Orgasms (2009)* by Michel Odent is a remarkable cutting-edge study on the human pleasure function in its largest contextual framework, and with special regard to female sexuality and the sexual function of birthing and breastfeeding. The study confirms and fully corroborates the earlier psychological, neurological and sociological research done by Wilhelm Reich, Herbert James Campbell, James W. Prescott, Ashley Montagu, and others.

The title of the book is deliberately coined to allude to Wilhelm Reich's pioneering study *The*

Function of the Orgasm (1942) as the author expressly notes, saying that his intention had been to 'rewrite *The Function of the Orgasm* in a new scientific context.'

Before I review this research more in detail, I may say this as an introduction. It is natural that one ventures out from one's own pleasure continuum. Everybody does that. For example, somebody who experiences homoerotic attraction, will venture out to know more about homosexuality, while someone who feels sexually attracted to the other sex will study the more conventional literature on love between the sexes.

In other words, the understanding of the whole of life, and the way we perceive life, is conditioned by how we experience pleasure. But it is also a limitative view when one ventures to know only about one's particular emotional or sexual addiction.

Michel Odent's approach is comparatively larger. While his focus is primarily upon *female sexuality* and the sexual nature of the process of birth, and breastfeeding, he is saying that the experience of pleasure, in its ecstatic dimension, connects us back with our source, and thus becomes an experience of transcendence, an experience that is not just

subjective and 'personal,' but essentially transpersonal.

Odent links back to the *oldest of traditions* that even Reich probably ignored, the times when women had freedom and power to live the whole of their feminine erotic experience. But now this is scientifically proven, not just a remembrance of olden times of matriarchy.

Odent's research is corroborated also by Candace Pert's discovery, back in the 1970s, of the opiate receptors, the so-called endorphins, the 'molecules of emotion,' as she called them.

—See Candace B. Pert, Molecules of Emotion (2003).

Odent's main tenet is that the female has been disempowered to give birth autonomously, because there is a fetus ejection reflex that is connected to the limbic system and the hypothalamus, and that is overridden by the neocortex. Hence, all kinds of procedures that 'assist' the mother in the birthing process are dysfunctional; all support, even midwifery, as Odent largely demonstrates, is dysfunctional as it activates the neocortex in the laboring woman and suppresses the fetus ejection reflex as a result. The same is true for the orgasmic experience of breastfeeding that was overridden,

according to the author, by guilt and shame as a result of cultural conditioning.

Odent also reports that the rise in cesarean birth led to mothers' lesser desire to breastfeed their infants, or to breastfeed only a short time. He advances evidence showing that breastfeeding should be a matter of years, not of months, with humans.

He also reports highly interesting details about certain apes and especially dolphins and their non-reproductive sexual life, which is based, as with humans, exclusively upon receiving pleasure and exchanging pleasure.

Besides, he speaks of a 'cocktail of love hormones' that is involved in any kind of sexual experience and a special hormone called *oxytocin* that triggers in the laboring woman a state of altered consciousness that leads to the mother ecstatically embracing the newborn with all her soul, making for deep bonding between mother and infant.

Needless to add that because of all birth assistance and machinery, the flow of those hormones has been largely blocked, which is the ultimate reason why women do no more like to breastfeed their infants, nor really bond with them in the first moments after

birth, which makes for later problems with parent-child codependence. I namely show in my extensive research findings on parent-child codependence and emotional abuse that one of the key factors in this etiology is lacking mother-infant symbiosis during the first eighteen months of the newborn, including a lack of breastfeeding and tactile care for the child from the part of the emotionally frigid and 'business addicted' mother.

Generally speaking, it is the inability of the mother to derive pleasure from the birthing and the post-birthing experience with the infant, and as a result of this blockage of the emotional flow, an ability of the mother to give to the baby a *sufficient amount of autonomy* to explore the world without the symbolic 'bondage' of the matrix.

When one grasps the *universality of pleasure* in the higher vertebrates and especially in the human, one's personal addiction loses importance and one ventures out into a larger realm of human experience that is valid and experienced by many more people than a tiny group. This then makes for a higher level of erotic intelligence and better overall judgment ability in matters of human emosexual experiences and their cognitive, emotional and social importance.

I have discovered *Eight Dynamic Patterns of Living* in the lifestyle of native peoples around the world, which are lifestyle patterns, or patterns of individual and collective behavior.

The first of this set of patterns is *autonomy*, the second is *ecstasy*. I also found that ecstasy is of paramount importance in the shamanic experience, and in deep healing.

Dr. Odent's research shows that besides the importance of the woman having full autonomy over her body during parturition, ecstasy is of high importance in the whole of human sexual life, and especially the experience of motherhood, with its high demand on being abundantly tactile with the child.

To fully understand the similarities between orgasmic states and other ecstatic states, we need to go far back in time, namely to the *Eastern Tantra*, a culture that preceded the pleasure-hostile *Vedanta* by thousands of years. While Vedanta is a relatively new religious paradigm in Hindu culture, Tantra was much longer-lived, and for good reasons.

Odent also cites the 'age of sacred prostitutes' and speaks about a *distorted scientific worldview* in which the main paradigms were forged only by men:

It is as if there are female ways to evaluate the comparative importance of different perspectives in exploring human nature. All scientific hypotheses are more or less based on intuitive knowledge and intuitive knowledge is gender related. Until recently the scientific world was highly dominated by men. We are entering a new phase in the history of sciences, with a more symmetrical input from each gender. (Id. 4)

From this insight into cultural bias, which is intrinsically a bias of perception, the author explains how it could happen that the fetus ejection reflex was overlooked for so long:

There are several reasons why we'll first look at the fetus ejection reflex. The first reason is that after thousands of years of culturally controlled birth very few people—including the natural childbirth advocates—can imagine what it is about. Another reason is that, in the current / scientific context, when the fetus ejection reflex is understood, it is easier to look at the other orgasmic/ecstatic states. We must add that this climax probably corresponds to the top of the highest possible ladder human beings may have the opportunity to climb. (Id., 4-5)

In accordance with the oldest religious teachings of the world, not only Tantra, but also Taoist doctrine and especially the teachings of Lao-tzu and

Chuang-tzu in China, Michel Odent advocates the *cultivation of sensuality* and *'orgasmic states'* as the ultimate pathway to transcendence, and the realization of unity with *all-that-is.*

It is wonderful to see a medical doctor, famous obstetrician, scientist and author of our days to have found this perennial wisdom that I equally dug out of the cultural treasure of the ancient wisdom traditions.

And equally in accordance with these traditions, Odent warns of the danger to overstimulate the neocortex through an exaggerated focus upon language, and concepts.

In all natural processes that require a let-go and an utmost of spontaneity, such as the sexual embrace and particularly, as the author shows, the birthing experience, the neocortex should be at rest, for otherwise it interferes with the quite automatic processes that nature has set in place for regulating and maintaining these processes in a sane manner. The author writes:

> An authentic fetus ejection reflex takes place when a human baby is born after a short series of irresistible contractions, which leave no room for voluntary movements. In such circumstances it is obvious that the neocortex (the part of the brain related to

intellectual activities) is at rest and no longer in control of the archaic brain structures in charge of vital functions such as giving birth. (Id., 9)

Michel Odent has summarized two decades of research done on spontaneous birthing, to demonstrate that when nature is followed, there is neither excruciating pain involved in giving birth to a child, nor any psychological symptoms that let birthing appear like a disease. We don't need to look back very far; still recently birthing was done in hospitals in pretty much the same way as operating a tumor, in *antiseptic rooms, under strong lights, with metallic instruments making sharp noise,* and with cameras installed for monitoring the 'operation.'

And I may add here, since I am living in South-East Asia since twenty years, that all those positive developments the author reports about the change of parturition toward a more 'homely' process, in a more home-like setting and ambience, has not taken place at all here in South-East Asia. It is here as it was in the West twenty or thirty years ago, with women giving birth to their children in an operation-hall kind of setting that is worse than anything before the advent of 'modern childbirth' in the West.

I may be allowed to report what I saw in a report on German television in my younger years, and thus already more than thirty years ago. That documentary was showing how women from a mountain tribe in Caucasia give birth under extreme conditions.

The film showed a strongly built woman walking naked into a mountain lake, at about −20° C. At the shore, a crowd of people was standing there in silence: her extended family and friends.

Walking ahead, she had to break the ice with her hands and feet, until she reached a spot that she found suitable for giving birth. She broke the ice in a circle around herself, and was then taking a position that in Chinese Kung Fu is called the 'horse' position, with her feet firmly on the ground, and her legs slightly bent, as if riding a horse. Then she seemed to get into a state of trance or meditation, as she suddenly was completely silent and immobile.

A few moments later her pelvis began to exhibit strong contractions, something like automatic convulsions that seemed to wanting to push the baby out.

And it was as one would expect it, as those pelvic contractions were very strong. It took no more than

about three of those major spams and the baby was falling out of her womb, in her hands, that she had held wide open, while bowing down with the last contraction. She took the newborn up, smiling, and bate through the umbilical cord. This was a matter of just seconds. Then she slowly and peacefully walked back to the shore where the crowd attended her in respectful silence.

This documentary fascinated me to a point that to this day I have not forgotten a single detail of it. And it of course came to mind right when reading Odent's book. It shows that, while the author makes believe that all tribal populations practice abusive and insane birthing rites, what the author claims to be a medical or obstetric novelty, is none. It has existed since millennia in tribal populations, while much of this wisdom is lost for our own culture, mainly through our patriarchal past.

The book also contains a professional and one would perhaps find, surprising, criticism of midwifery. But the argument is not far-fetched when we see that any kind of assistance or 'coaching' may suggest to the laboring woman that she is not in control of the process, but that other people are, who are 'professionals.' The author writes:

Understanding that laboring women need to feel secure, without feeling observed and judged, leads us to the root of midwifery. It seems that women have always had a tendency to give birth close to their mother, or occasionally close to an experienced mother who could fulfill the role of a mother figure: the midwife was originally a mother figure and, in an ideal world, our mother is the prototype of the person with whom one can feel secure without feeling observed, or judged. In most societies, though, the role of the midwife has been gradually altered. Most languages condition women to accept that they do not have the power to give birth by themselves; they must 'be delivered' by somebody. As a result, the midwife has gradually become a figure who is more often than not an authoritarian and dominating guide, an observer, and an agent of the cultural milieu. She has also played a key role in the transmission of perinatal beliefs and rituals. (Id., 11)

The fetus ejection reflex can also be inhibited by vaginal examinations, eye-to-eye contact or by the imposition of a change of environment, as would happen when a woman is transferred to a delivery room. It is inhibited when the intellect of the laboring woman is stimulated by any sort of rational language, for example if the birth attendant says: 'No you are at complete dilation. It's time to push.' In other words, any interference tends to bring the laboring woman 'back down to Earth' and tends to transform the fetus

ejection reflex into a second stage of labor which involves involuntary movements. (Id., 12-13)

In addition, there is another important key element in the birthing process that was traditionally overlooked in our medical tradition. It is the hidden truth about how the mother bonds with the newborn, and what the mechanisms are of this bonding.

This was notoriously a matter fervently discussed in religious and transcendental circles, as science was saying since quite a few decades that no mother loves her newborn 'automatically' but that there must be something like a mutual kind of adoption.

This was also what psychoanalysis is saying and what, for example, Françoise Dolto (1908–1988) was telling me in an interview back in 1986 about the matter. Of course, while in those circles this scientific view was debated, the great public, following religion, believed that 'naturally, all mothers love their babies.' What is true here, and what is myth, we may ask? Michel Odent shows that both views are somehow true, depending on how we define 'love.' Nature has not overlooked this important clue as most cultures have. It is namely through the same 'cocktail of love hormones' that the author says makes

birth a natural and easy process, that mother-infant bonding occurs immediately after birth.

Candace B. Pert would call it a matter involving the 'molecules of emotion.' The author writes:

> There are clear similarities between the immediate post orgasmic states following a fetus ejection reflex and an orgasm of genital sexuality. During the hour following the birth, when mother and newborn baby are in close skin-to-skin contact and have not yet eliminated the hormones released during the ejection reflex, each of these hormones has a specific role to play—natural morphine being a typical example. Since all opiates have the properties necessary to create states of dependency, it seems obvious that body-to-body contact between two individuals who are under the effects of endorphins can induce the beginning of a co-dependency, or in other worlds of an attachment. (Id., 45)

Finally, the author emphasizes the importance of extended breastfeeding, which is not only a concern for bringing up infants within a continuum of utmost tactile stimulation and optimum nutrition, but also a concern of public sanity.

As we have seen above, James W. Prescott showed in more than twenty years of research on the roots of violence that the turndown of breastfeeding within

violent tribal cultures, ancient patriarchy, and modern consumer culture is one of the primary factors in the etiology of violence.

—James W. Prescott, Body Pleasure and the Origins of Violence (1975), Deprivation of Physical Affection as a Primary Process in the Development of Physical Violence, A Comparative and Cross-Cultural Perspective, in: David G. Gil, ed., Child Abuse and Violence (1979), Affectional Bonding for the Prevention of Violent Behaviors, Neurobiological, Psychological and Religious/Spiritual Determinants, in: Hertzberg, L.J., Ostrum, G.F. and Field, J.R., (Eds.), Violent Behavior, Vol. 1, Assessment & Intervention, Chapter Six (1990), The Origins of Human Love and Violence, Pre- and Perinatal Psychology Journal, Volume 10, Number 3: Spring 1996, pp. 143–188, Prevention or Therapy and the Politics of Trust: Inspiring a New Human Agenda, in: Psychotherapy and Politics International, Volume 3(3), pp. 194–211 (2005).

Michel Odent writes:

The duration of breastfeeding is undoubtedly influenced by family structures. Since human societies organize mating and create marriage rules, they also indirectly influence the duration of breastfeeding. Nobody knows exactly what the physiological ideal for the duration of breastfeeding is among humans. For any other mammal, the answer is simple—almost as simple as for the duration of pregnancy. For example, after spending 230 days in the womb, the baby chimpanzee is fed by its mother for two years; a bottle-nosed dolphin is breastfed for 16 months. For human beings the answer is much more imprecise, although a physiological ideal can be deduced as a reference point. Comparing human beings with other

mammals and taking into account the duration of our life in the womb, our degree of maturity at birth, our lifespan, the special nutritional needs of our big brain, tooth development, and so forth, we might conclude that breastfeeding among humans was originally maintained for a matter of years rather than a few months. (Id., 66-67)

The author also clarifies on page 67 that before the 'lifelong strict monogamy,' most babies were breastfed for two to four years, which was a practice that according to the author started in ancient Greece and went along all the way up until the 19th century —and I may add here that in the upper classes of most societies, this is still the case today, and was so in my own family.

My grandmother did not breastfeed any one of her four children. This was done by the 'Amme,' a maid specially hired for that purpose, who had time and love for this work. What this truth suggests is that we need to be precise about the words we are using.

When we talk about responsible parenting, this does not imply that parents are not replaceable. They are to a certain extent.

What children need is caretakers even if they are not their parents! While in most cases these roles are

both met by the parents of the child, this does not need to be so!

The important thing here is that the child's needs are met, first of all their bodily needs, then as a matter of culture, also their mental and intellectual needs.

In agreement with Riane Eisler who wrote in her book *Sacred Pleasure (1996)* that pre-patriarchal cultures such as the ancient *Minoan Civilization* were essentially sane and peaceful because they respected the natural laws of nature, including the natural equality between male and female, I would go on to say that in our attempt to formulate new and better social policies, we need to *emphasize pleasure,* because it is pleasure that turns down violence, and only pleasure, and that means that we have to understand 'orgasmic states' as the real pathways to transcendence, not just as a form of individual or social entertainment. In a way, the quest for reinstituting the natural pleasure function in all its dimensions is a holy, sacred quest because life, and all natural life functions, and especially sexuality, are sacred.

Michel Odent gives conclusive examples out of the life of the higher apes and dolphins that demonstrate that these animals, that are the most closely

genetically related to the human race, do enjoy a sexual life that is non-reproductive.

This research is really important for it shows the *invalidity of the view forwarded by fundamentalist religions* that sexuality was exclusively procreative in the whole of the animal realm, and that only humans have 'transgressed' this 'natural law' by being 'pansexual' to the utmost extent. In fact, the argument of 'pansexuality' is turned down by 'Christian' scientists such as Jeffrey Satinover who attack not only homosexuality but also pedophilia, if not the whole range of sexual paraphilias with the blissfully ignorant argument that with mammals sexuality was *highly regulated and procreation-focused*, not pleasure focused.

— Jeffrey Satinover, Homosexuality and the Politics of Truth (1996).

Much to the contrary, Dr. Odent writes:

Dolphins are known to have sex very frequently, in many different ways, for reasons other than reproduction, and they sometimes engage in acts of a homosexual nature. Copulation takes place face-to-face and though many species of dolphins engage in lengthy foreplay, the actual act is usually only brief, but may be repeated several times within a short time span. Various dolphin species have even been known

to engage in sexual behavior with other dolphin species. Occasionally, dolphins will also show sexual behavior towards other animals, including humans. (Id., 90)

[Bonobos] often copulate face-to-face and the frontal orientation of the Bonobo vulva and clitoris both strongly suggest that the female genitalia are adapted for this position. During sexual intercourse the females have been heard emitting grunts and squeals that probably reflect orgasmic experiences, which perhaps explains why sex, among bonobos, is not just for reproduction—it is the key to their social life. Bonobos become sexually aroused remarkably easily, and they express this excitement in a variety of mounting positions and forms of genital contact. Perhaps the bonobo's most typical sexual pattern is genito-genital rubbing between adult females. The two females rub their genital swellings laterally together. Male bonobos, too, may engage in pseudocopulation; they often perform a back to back variation, one male briefly rubbing his scrotum against the buttocks of another. These mammals also practice so-called penis fencing, in which two males hang face-to-face from a branch, rubbing their erect penises together. (Id., 90-91)

Michel Odent emphasizes the fact that humans have genetically tight relations with aquatic animals, a fact that has been overlooked by philosophers and scholars for thousands of years. It is also significant,

the author reports, that human babies can stay erect and walk in water before they are able to walk on dry land. Dr. Odent then concludes on page 94 that 'all chapters of human anatomy, physiology, behavior, pathology, and evolutionary medicine must be rewritten in the light of this so-called 'aquatic-ape theory.'

I wish that this important book finds an audience beyond the circles of academia, which has unfortunately never happened with the research both of Herbert James Campbell and James W. Prescott, as the mass media appear to suppress any such information these days for reasons of *'political correctness,'* at least as far the United States of America is concerned.

Nonetheless, as this is a vital and noble cause, especially when we think of reformulating the basic social policies that regulate human behavior, and specifically those that regulate human sexuality, we must grant this research a prime agenda for it unveils most of the myths that cultural conditioning has brought up about the nature of pleasure, thereby belittling or outright turning down the importance of pleasure for the human race, and generally, for all of life. We also should keep in mind that *cutting-edge*

quantum physics and consciousness research demonstrated that even particles *possess consciousness* and actually choose where they wish to be and in which orbits they wish to circulate around the nucleus.

In a sense, we can say that it is up to them where they are located, until the moment they are observed, and thus localize; however without observation, they may determine their locality as a matter of pleasure.

We have good reasons to assume that the pleasure function is not restricted to human beings alone, but that all of creation basically 'runs on pleasure,' which means that positive sensations are the stimulus for evolution, for life to unfold. It is deplorable that over the last five thousand years, and with the turn of Tantra into Vedanta, and the historical turn to devolution, the pleasure function was demonized in a way that is unprecedented in human evolutionary history.

This namely led to forging laws that are punishing life, and that are countering the positive evolution of humanity.

There cannot be an evolution of the human race, and generally, of all of life, as long as we *demonize and*

prohibit pleasure, or when we regard human sexuality as basically dangerous and potentially aggressive.

Our criminal laws, and particularly our sex laws do not display much respect of the human nature; in fact they seem to consider us to be an 'impossible human' instead of a 'possible human,' which is why these laws need to be abolished.

For anyone engaged in law reform and the necessary reform of our basic social policies, the scientific contribution Michel Odent has made is substantial and important. It is important because it shows that the natural pleasure function is in no way to be taken as a 'potentially chaotic behavior' but is regulated by nature in a way that no harm is done.

When harm is done, it is not the result of the natural pleasure function, but the *turndown of that function* through moralism and fundamentalist life-denial.

Proposal 10/12

We were looking at research that demonstrates the importance of pleasure, and the role of the pleasure function, in the natural human setup. We saw that this research fully confirms not religion, but secular concepts which since long intuited that the human being is not by nature violent, but that violence is a conditioned response.

We also saw that research proved that pleasure and violence are in a mutually exclusive relationship, by the very infrastructure of our brain, which means that when pleasure is on, violence is off, and when pleasure is off, violence is on. We further saw that pleasure enhances intelligence, while violence reduces intelligence, that pleasure helps building the necessary *preferred pathways,* that is, neuronal connections, as early as in childhood, but not only in childhood, that make both for high intelligence and a nonviolent, peaceful lifestyle.

It can thus be said that patriarchy with its horrendous fear of pleasure and its repressive attitude toward pleasure, as well as all religions that have supported patriarchy, are responsible for our society being so violent. Our society being violent means

both that the human beings in this society are predominantly violent in their overall behavior, and that the society, its institutions, its police forces, and its law enforcement procedures, are structurally violent.

At the same time both the majority of humans in our society, and its social institutions are hardly aware of their violence, and tend to play this fact down, belittle it or project it on certain social groupings, on certain groups called 'sex offenders' or the generic group of 'criminals,' those 'behind bars,' those who are labeled for their particular kind of violence or nonviolence, those who have smoked 'illegal plants,' those who have touched a child in 'illegal ways,' and so on and so forth.

The very vocabulary that this society uses for *labeling people and discarding them out* from the group, to let them roast years and decades in its endless prison miles is a signal for how mad, how truly insane this society is.

It is obvious, after we have seen the hidden or not so hidden connections between pleasure and violence, and between pleasure and intelligence that the only valid social policy for bringing about a more peaceful

society is to do away with all pleasure-denying policies, including draconian sex laws, and to *enhance the pleasure function* as early as in childhood, through fostering a really permissive education, a love education.

I may add a word here on the status quo. It is certainly not surprising that under the absolutist regime of the Church, the human pleasure function was turned down, as it is also proven now by research on the relationship between sexual activity and identity, that when people are deprived of sexual mating, they are losing identity and become dull and passive, that is, easy to regulate and to rule around. Dictators intuited this fact since millennia and in all fascist regimes, pleasures are turned down and violence is screwed up, sexual behavior is severely restricted and all but procreative sexual behavior is demonized and harshly punished.

All this we know, or let's say, those who have kept their pleasure function intact, know it, while those who are already on the violence track, tend to persistently deny it.

My question is how it can happen that a secular state such as a modern democracy has taken over this

fatally wrong social policymaking, while such a state doesn't really want to rule around its citizens, doesn't really want to indoctrinate them with severely ethical restrictions, doesn't really want to establish a political dictatorship?

Yet perhaps without deliberate reflection, this insane tool box has been taken over from the dark ages, including the absolutely insane sex laws.

And not only that, after having taken all this over, the modern state even goes on to expand those outmoded dysfunctional sex laws to make them even more severe, and *direct them against children and adolescents* who are now considered as potential 'sex offenders.' If this is not state-ordained paranoia, I don't know what it is!

But I am not even sure that the incentives are set directly by government officials, and I even doubt it.

It is in my experience much more plausible that behind this trend to *legal fascism* are the churches and sects, and religious fundamentalism, and our control-obsessed multinationals.

I must leave the question open here for it goes beyond the scope of this proposal, which is meant to be scientific and not political in the strict sense of the

term, and which sees no good in labeling and accusing certain people or groups of people for what appears to be institutionalized insanity.

The question remains, while there may be a number of perhaps contradictory answers. The question is why, despite democracy, and secular states, insanity is perpetuated over generations, and why no change was so far brought about?

It is true that there were attempts to reform the system including reform of the age of consent laws, back in the 1970s. But from about the mid 80s, the opposite trend set in that was to wipe all reform ideas from the table, to re-establish the antiquated form of holding the citizen tight and rule him or her around in all possible ways. Certain plants were declared illegal, harmless forms of adult-child touch were declared 'a crime,' let alone sexual relations between both groups.

The touch alone suffices now to get somebody jailed for twenty years. If such is not insane as a social policy, especially now, as we have the scientific proof that all touch is beneficial and even important for the healthy growth of the child, I do not know what is insane!

From the mid 80s, the abuse culture, as a form of institutionalized insanity, was brought about, with all the consequences we are facing today.

The main consequences are a general rise of domestic, sexual and structural violence, the rise of police violence, the rise of violence against social, sexual and ethnic minorities, a rise of violence beyond the borders of the state, through international hegemonic strategies, and other deplorable social factors such as a rise of youth suicide, the rise of addictions of all kinds, the rise of depression, the rise of terminal diseases such as heart disease, cancer or immune deficiency syndrome, and a rise of exactly the sexual tendencies that the state wants to see turned down, that is, homosexuality, pedophilia, and large-scale sadomasochism.

Is that surprising? No, it's not, it is the paradoxical answer of nature.

As quantum physics has shown conclusively, nature answers with paradoxes when we look at nature in the wrong way, when our concepts about nature are dysfunctional, when our belief system about natural behavior is flawed. *Quid est demonstrandum.*

11/12

Male Affection as a Peace Conduit

Homoemotional Affection gets Males into Balance.
Homosexual Attraction gets Males out of Balance.

Developing affection between males, which includes males of different generations is of paramount importance for reducing violence in our society.

There is no doubt that males are the ones who are primarily responsible for most of the violence committed on a daily basis in any given society—and I may add, not just males, but emotionally confused males.

What is the emotional confusion that many males are suffering from? It is the idea that yin-values, tenderness, caregiving behaviors, and bonding, to name a few, are somehow reserved for women only.

Of course, this emotional distortion is by no means a result of nature, but a consequence of culture, wrong culture, which induces in men this kind of simplistic and overly restrictive self-definition.

It goes without saying that males are just as eager as females for delivering care, especially care for the young.

When males suppress this natural desire, they suffer emotionally, on a subconscious level, and this suffering contributes to their becoming violent.

This desire to be caring is natural and is related to the *pleasure of being naked and vulnerable* in the presence of those one loves, the partner, and one's children, and sharing one's affection through fondling, stroking and hugging.

These are natural behaviors that are known in all societies all over the world, but males who struggle with restrictive cultural norms will tend to avoid them, belittle them, ridicule them or declare them as 'unnatural.'

Affection, shared tenderness, where sexual attraction is not excluded but largely secondary, is the most natural of all behaviors. Males can exhibit such affection toward elders, children, other males and, in moments of the day where mating is inappropriate, with their partner. What I am saying here is that one of these affectionate relations is more important than the others, more important not generally, but in our

specific culture. It is male-male affection, and the affection of senior males to junior males, both in the corporate and outside the corporate setting.

Within the corporate setting, friendship and mutual support between senior and junior managers are daily reality. These relations form part of our positive ethical code.

They are largely approved and subsequently supported by the social framework; they do not encounter suspicion or estrangement. But outside of the corporate setting, things look a bit more wild, and a bit less protected. The social framework seems to only marginally support such relations.

When a male spends much of his time with another male, outside of the corporate setting, there is often suspicion the men were either homosexuals or, while being heterosexuals, were for one time interested in a homosexual affair.

Typically, things do not turn out that way, not naturally so, in my observation. The desire for affectionate bonding is real between males, and it is of the utmost importance for emotional balance in males.

This kind of bonding may at times be homoemotional in the sense that such exchanges may include nonsexual gestures such as hugging, pat on the back or shoulder, slap on the butt as sometimes observed among teammates in various sports, and lastly perhaps even a kiss on the cheek.

There may also be shared nudity, but *no sexual mating* in the sense of genital interaction.

In such a case, we cannot speak of homosexuality or homoerotic behavior. I am speaking in such cases of 'homoemotional bonding.'

This kind of bonding between males, this is the interesting thing, reinforces the sexual attraction of males toward females, because emotional balance is necessary in males for being fully attracted to females. To put it in a shorter formula, homoemotional bonding reinforces heterosexual behavior and attraction.

Now let us look at the homosexual scenario, which looks quite different. Here we encounter males who are out of touch with their yin nature, and equally out of touch with their natural behavior pattern to bond affectionately with other males. Now what fills this vacuum then is *compulsive sexual mating*, where

'sexual' means the genital embrace in either the positive-master-phallic role or the negative-slave-vulva role.

Here, we see not two full human males bond but two oversexed bodies copulate where one is reduced to a sperm-giving phallus and the other to a sperm-receiving oral or anal vulva.

Research on homosexuality shows that men who suffer from homosexual attraction are out of balance, go out for mating with a large number of different partners, in unsafe places like public toilets, and may, as psychiatrist Jeffrey Satinover, in his book *Homosexuality and the Politics of Truth (1996)* shows with an example, have up to about fifteen different partners in one single night.

I concede that Satinover's book is written from a slightly *homophobic* base position and an outspokenly 'Christian' moral inhibition against this form of mating, a bias I do not personally share.

The book has however its value, when one is able to accept the author's position as a simple form of respect for his personal opinion and his perhaps bewildered feelings.

The person that Satinover talks about in his book was one of his immune deficiency syndrome patients when he was still a practicing psychiatrist, and the man died atrociously a few months later.

I doubt that all homosexuals live their love in such a compulsive manner, but some of them may. There are many who live in stable relationships.

Strangely enough, while Satinover's concern regarding the etiology of AIDS seems rational when we are looking at single males who go out for unsafe copulations virtually every night, and in many different places, this doesn't seem to be the case with homosexuals who live in stable partner relations.

Yet Satinover says that AIDS in these cases is not lesser than with the first group of homosexual males. This argument, which is not backed by scientific evidence, cannot be verified rationally.

So I may forward my own observations and experiences instead, while I am, exactly like Satinover, not a member of the homosexual community, nor am I in any way anti-homosexuality. Thus I have no bias.

I may not have all the information needed, however, and I am ready to admit that. But I have encountered homosexuals and have always attracted

homosexuals when looking for a (female) partner through placing an ad in MSN. I got about fifty replies, and about 10% were homosexuals. However, the way they behaved estranged me.

As I have no prejudice against homosexuality, and found especially one of those males interesting, I proposed a friendship. The man was a lawyer, like myself, from Rome, Italy and wrote a perfect English —obviously an intelligent and cultivated man. He invited me on the spot to come to see him in Rome and spend a fortnight with him. However, when I replied I would like to visit Rome again and improve my Italian, visit his law firm, and have discussions with him and affectionate exchanges, he was reacting with outright estrangement, and a kind of ultimatum. He simply replied that either I would come to have sex with him, or not come.

As I replied in the same calm manner that I was not homosexual but could well imagine an interesting friendship with him, I got silence as a reply. And with the other four homosexuals, from South America, the scenario was the same, while communication was certainly not a problem, as I speak and write Spanish.

In my view, such behavior is compulsive!

As a heterosexual, I have many friendships with women and cannot imagine to be categorical in such a manner, as we need both passionate relations and affectionate relations. In times of crisis, I often saw in my life that friendships are more important than passionate love relations, as they provide emotional stability and support, and thereby are a balancing factor in all times of turmoil.

Hence, to discard such relations out from one's life may be a signal that the person is emotionally imbalanced. Affectionate relations are as important if not more important than passionate love relations. This is so because affection and tenderness are balancing emotions.

Now, the most interesting while in many societies also the most critically disputed kind of relations is those between adult males and young boys. I am advocating to consider that those relations may not always be pederastic, but are in my view, for the most part, and naturally so, platonic in the sense that the sexual impulse is sublimated if not on both ends of the relation, but certainly on the side of the adult. I have demonstrated such a relation in a fictive tale, a teaching tale, I wrote in the form of a film that features and illustrates the affectionate bonding

between a Frenchman, David, and a 12-year old Jewish boy, Jonathan, in Paris.

David had been in a monastery before because of pedophile relations with boys, and as a result had to cope with strong feelings of guilt and shame that induced in him the desire to retreat from society, lucky enough to not have suffered criminal prosecution. But he had taken a firm vow to not fall back in the old pattern. So he keeps the relation with Jonathan strictly affectionate and refuses all erotic advances of the boy, who for that reason, flees him during a nightly train travel, to be picked up by a pedophile artist and filmmaker who sleeps with him that very night, much to the boy's gratification as he missed exactly that aspect in the relationship with David.

When they later discuss the affair, the boy concedes that he loves David more than Jim, the filmmaker, because of shared values which are beyond the merely physical aspect of the relation. The film was actually inspired by the Biblical story of 'David and Jonathan' where David talks about his love for the boy as 'surpassing all woman love.'

I wanted to show in this film that men-boy relations, while their sexual aspect has been subject to scientific study, are not defined by that sexual aspect but rather by the variety of nonsexual affectionate interactions and values that are typically part of such relations.

—See Theo Sandfort, The Sexual Aspect of Pedophile Relations: The Experience of Twenty-five Boys (1982).

It has been found even by mainstream psychologists that male affection is for adolescent boys even more important than for adult men. To receive affection and support from older males is a constituting factor in the psychosexual growth of young boys.

James W. Prescott, whom I mentioned earlier on, also advocates intergenerational affectionate bonding as a constituting factor in brain development toward nonviolence and caring, nurturant behaviors.

Dr. Prescott emphasized in private communication that such affectionate bonding is in no way to be confused with pederasty or pedophilia, as in most cases the adult partners restrain their sexual impulse either because of the law or of cultural factors that determine these relations to be affectionate only.

I can confirm this view from my cross-cultural experience. Having lived and worked in many different cultures, I can testify that for example in South-East Asia, despite the common prejudice of these cultures being sexually abusive toward children, the rule is that adult-child bonding is affectionate only, as the traditional morality strongly opposes adult-child sexual bonding.

There is well in my observation physical abuse in the form of adult-child harsh chastisement, but I have not seen any circumstances or situations involving sexual abuse. I am talking here of course only about local people relating to each other, not the largely discussed affairs between foreigners and local children that are on the agenda of most NGOs and that have for that reason been widely eradicated.

In fact, nonviolent and affectionate bonding is the rule in Asia between males and young children of both sexes, not only in the school setting but everywhere. Male Asians are not suspecting other males being sexually intended in any way when interacting with a child, while this seems today to be a group fantasy in all Western cultures, to a point it has reached the level of public hysteria.

I have heard many stories of real child protection in Asia, while when we follow the news, the contrary seems to be true for most Western countries. It is not uncommon in Asia that children have to walk or bike to their school a few miles every day, without being accompanied by anybody.

Here in Phnom Penh, Cambodia, where I am living since more than ten years, small children of three to five years walk in the streets without any apparent protection, barely dressed or even completely naked; they cross streets, they buy their candies at kiosks, they have their friends and relationships, but there is well an invisible protection simply because everybody cares for any child, not just for one's own child.

And it is very rare to see a child get lost.

I have heard of only one or two such cases in the ten years I live here, and in both cases, the child was taken back to the family by caring adults other than the parents who were investigating the issue, without any police needed, and taking the right action to get the child back to the family. In most cases, the loss of children is not related to abduction for sexual purposes, but for a variety of other reasons, or

because the child simply wanted to visit a distant relative and had no idea how far it actually was to get there.

Adult-child affectionate bonding is of paramount importance for reducing violence in our society. The media's perverse focus on child abduction and child pornography is unreasonable as it is not conducive to really building a safe environment for our children.

As I have extensively analyzed the situation, I can only say that child protection is no protection. If anything, it is another consumer business, and more specifically, a global business. There are big corporations earning a lot of money with that, while this whole absurd theater has done absolutely nothing to give real safety to our children.

The mass media around the world uniformly keep repeating that in matters of child protection, the situation is getting worse with every year, to come, despite all the government funding for new and better child protective measures, most of them being highly coercive, many of them infringing upon civil rights; and yet the effectiveness of this whole machinery is close to zero! The challenge for new policy making in this area in our Western civilizations

is obvious. We are struggling with a problem that, as it all boils down to, we don't really understand. We are trying to fight an enemy that we don't really know. We are screwing up our laws every year, and turn down civil liberties accordingly because things are going in the wrong way, but we don't know why they are going in the wrong way.

Sergio Zyman, former CEO of the Coca Cola Company writes in his enlightening book *The End of Marketing (2000)* that when you run a promotion and evaluate the results, you may believe you have been successful because of your promotion while in many cases, the reason why you were successful had nothing to do with the promotion and was based upon factors you ignored at that moment. Of course, when you run the next promotion based on the same false premises you most likely will fail because of your perception bias.

Hence, the lesson to learn here is that life is too complex to be reduced to one cause bringing about one effect; the reality is that one cause brings about multiple effects, and one single effect may be brought about by many causes.

Until the day our politicians learn that not a Cartesian but only a holistic approach to reality will ensure they are drafting the right social policies, we are going to continue to stumble in the mess with no results delivered other than *a massive police empire* that jails and discards more of its citizens with every coming year.

The digestive tube of these insane social policies ends in endless prison miles where a large portion of our society is given over to an *unpredictable fate* while they are humans just like all of us.

This process needs to be reversed.

Social policies need to be drafted that reduce crime effectively at the root level, that is, through real prevention, not through endless persecutions and prosecutions.

The bulldog police state that needs zillions of police is 'on very shaky ground,' observes the American career coach Laurence G. Boldt in his book *The Tao of Abundance (1999)*. In fact, it is not grounded at all, it floats in the air with the feet above the head, as the Fool of the Tarot. It is a puer culture that is characterized by its abysmal *collective narcissism* as a result of all the traumata inflicted upon children

185

through all the fear and terror that both the family and the state inflict upon the tiniest member of the community.

It has to be brought to the International Court of Justice that in the United States of America children are registered as sex offenders, and are being lynched or electrocuted simply for living their sex life. If Congress does nothing to abolish these laws, Congress *will be forced to do so by a higher instance.*

I am hopeful that human rights lawyers around the world will be more and more sensitive to these issues and will take appropriate action!

Of course, this undesirable result can be avoided if a responsible government steers a different course, simply by intelligently understanding that the current way of doing leads straight into an impasse.

Proposal 11/12

In today's modern society, the immense progress made by the Gay-Lesbian movement seems, on the surface, to be the hallmark of the free world. However, in reality, social benefits granted to the gay community constitute the stopping point with respect to freedom. In other words, the achievements of the gay movement are as far as society will go in terms of granting social accommodations!

—See already John P. Alston & Francis Tucker, The Myth of Sexual Permissiveness, The Journal of Sex Research 9/1 (1973).

In older, traditional societies, homosexuality may not be embraced, it may even be ridiculed, but these societies give way more freedom, including sexual freedom, to their children. Field research carried out as early as in the 1920s by Bronislaw Malinowski and Margaret Mead on the Trobriand natives in Melanesia showed that in this culture, homosexuality, pedophilia and sexual crime are virtually unknown.

—See, for example, Bronislaw Malinowski, Crime and Custom in Savage Society (1926), Sex and Repression in Savage Society (1927) and The Sexual Life of Savages in North West Melanesia (1929) as well as Margaret Mead, Sex and Temperament in Three Primitive Societies (1935).

In addition, Trobriands are almost ideal marriage partners. Marriages tend to last long if not for life, and the divorce rate is about 3 to 4% only. The reason why these reputed anthropologists found this tribal culture to that point sane and balanced was that these natives give their children an utmost degree of love, freedom, autonomy and respect, which includes sexual freedom.

Children are never punished, never beaten, and spoken to softly and in a way to show them they are 'big enough' to understand.

When a child was naughty, a parent would simply talk seriously with the boy or girl and the child would listen, and correct their behavior.

From about age 3, children sleep together in special dormitories. One of the reasons for this custom is that Trobriands are naturally afraid of parent-child incest, which is the primary reason for this tradition.

The second reason is that Trobriands believe that children are naturally promiscuous before they reach puberty. Hence, there is freedom for these children to copulate with each other, while it's usually the older

children who initiate the younger ones for love making.

Interestingly so, when a child reaches puberty, their sexual behavior changes completely. There is no more promiscuity, but the child searches for a partner, a person for sharing all their emotional and sexual life, a durable relationship. After some such long-term relationships, somewhere between age 15 and 18, then, Trobriands marry and have a highly regulated family life. There is no more promiscuity, and there is no mistress-keeping either.

When we look at research on homosexuality and especially newer research on pedophilia as I have myself conducted it, we see that the *etiology of pedophilia clearly is a childhood hangup*. It is through lacking peer-peer relations, or disturbed relations that the person, usually either at the end of adolescence, or in their thirties, suddenly realizes an attraction toward children. This attraction, as it is to be seen in many personal stories, is first not sexual at all, but emotional. It is as if the adult wanted to be again a child, at least in the imaginal realm, hence the need to be around children, to play with children, to be childish and to engage in dependency relations.

In most cases, these *dependency relations* are really falling in the pattern of pathological codependence, thereby repeating what the pedophile man or woman went through as a child, as they regularly have had highly codependent parents. It is usually the relationship with the parent of the opposite sex that is the problematic one where codependence was the reason for the child or adolescent to be deprived of peer relations, and thus to be deprived of early emotional and sexual freedom.

As a result, this early deprivation of autonomy is later a vacuum that the person needs to fill. It is filled through *codependent relations with children* who then, psychologically, play the role of the parent who did 'not give enough love.' The child or adolescent is then in the pedophile relation the 'healing agent,' which is why in my view, pedophilia is always a temporary condition, not as the myth goes, a lifelong addiction.

In addition, I have shown in various publications that the 'pedophile predator' as it ghosts around in our mass media today, is a myth.

But one thing should be clear-cut for our policymakers. It is the fact that it is our society itself that breeds large-scale homosexuality, lesbianism and

pedophilia! The reason is wrong education of our small children, which is largely violent, lacking out in true respect for children, both from the side of parents and educators, the belittling of children as being 'childish and immature,' the lack of honesty that talks 'over the head' of children instead of talking with them as fully equal persons, and the *commercial exploitation* of children through mass media manipulation.

Hence, the only reasonable solution to these distortions of nature, or social pathologies, is the establishment of a truly permissive education.

12/12

Fostering Permissive Education

Promoting the Cause of the Sexual Child is not Pedophilia.
Pedophilia is Not a Social Cause but a Psychosexual Hangup.

Developing an argument for permissiveness is not easy in a society that is highly controlled and that *believes in control* more than it believes in self-regulation.

Nature is based upon self-regulation, not control, upon flow, not upon coercion, upon co-evolving systems, not upon conflicting systems.

—See, for example, Fritjof Capra, The Systems View of Life: A Unifying Vision (2014) with further references.

There are certain social philosophies and scientific doctrines that I do not need to name here, as this is common knowledge, philosophies that made us believe that society is a creative mess that needs antagonism as the motor for all to run smoothly. It is a belief system that views human aggression as normal as civil war, and reasons that without aggression there would be no evolution.

It is a belief system, sometimes called *Social Darwinism,* that sees violence as 'imbedded in human nature' and that assumes that societies in a way need to be violent and destroy themselves so that there is renewal in nature, and renewal in culture.

Oswald Spengler, an author who by the way was not putting too much effort in distancing himself from the Nazi ideology, was forwarding such a view.

Darwinism contributed to this view by stating that random mutations are the rule, while complex order was the exception in nature.

During Darwin's lifetime, science ignored that nature is basically consisting of *entangled autopoietic networks that are mutually self-sustaining and co-evolving.*

When we look at modern systems theory, where is the violence that these scientific and social freaks have believed to be 'inherent in nature'?

The truth is there is no such violence to be found in living systems. What is to be found is intelligent patterned order, total information, and something like total care for the sustainability of the system, which is an effect, as we know today, of the quantum field, the

quantum scale or unified field, in which all living beings are interconnected.

Those philosophies are simply invalid. Fritjof Capra has done a major intellectual effort in demonstrating in several of his books that Darwinism *is systemically wrong and out as a science paradigm* as it largely represents a projection upon nature, not the result of an observation of nature.

—See Fritjof Capra, The Web of Life (1997), The Hidden Connections (2002) and The Systems View of Life (2014).

And with regard to Spengler and Toynbee, who notoriously predicted the 'Fall of Civilizations' as an automatism in human evolution, they were of course examining *highly violent patriarchal civilizations* that, because of their abysmal violence, had to suffocate in that violence as a matter of karma, as a simple matter of cause and effect. But their wrong conclusion is to assume an automatism in all societies that makes that one day they will decay. This assumption simply has not been verified scientifically in any way.

In ancient China, before the times of the *Warring States*, the time namely of King Wen, author of the I Ching, there were kingdoms that lasted over many generations because their rulers were nonviolent and

wistful. They were studying the Tao (Way), they were treating their vassals not as vassals, but as full humans, and they were respecting the human nature. As a result, their lawmaking was smooth and permissive.

It was exactly the Warring States, the subsequent period that is very closely related to our modern consumerist mass culture, which was characterized by political and moral decadence, the upcoming of moralism as a coercive mandatory set of rules, and draconian laws that was then, not long thereafter, decaying within all the abysmal violence it had created for itself and other kingdoms.

It was this kind of 'Armageddon' culture that was later ruthlessly annihilated by those it had repeatedly raped and violated in its conquests all over China, just as it was the case, in the West, with the Assyrian patriarchs and King Hammurabi, the creator of the first compulsive penal law known in the history of human sexual behavior.

To state that giving the child free choice relations, the freedom to maintain their friendships, be have sensual, erotic and sexual exchanges would amount to 'normalizing pedophilia' is on the same line of

reasoning. For it assumes that violence is somehow embedded in all human sexuality and that an adult partner will always represent potential danger to a child who is enamored with that adult. It is on the same line of *violent moralism* that is so characteristic for upside-down cultures, for highly decadent cultures, to assume that every adult facing a naked child is driven to rape and assault the child.

This is clearly a projection, not an observation of nature or of human behavior. It is to assume that *psychopathological behavior* is the rule for humans, while it is clearly the exception.

Psychopathological behavior is to an extent daily reality in our modern consumer cultures that it strikes the observer for this is completely unknown in cultures that are still closer to nature.

The best example is Japan, a culture that was basically sane traditionally, still today having one of the lowest incidences of heart disease, cancer or immune deficiency syndrome, mainly as a result of their nutritional wisdom, and the fact that sexual behavior was never condemned in their culture as sinful, except with regard to homosexuality.

And yet, since Hiroshima and Nagasaki, the Japanese have sought to be close with American culture and tried to model and clone American lifestyle to the utmost extent this is possible for an Asian.

The result is that today, Japan has next to Australia one of the highest youth suicide rates in the world and psychopathological incidents like the mass shooting of children in schools by mad youngsters are daily reality, just as in the United States or France.

As long as our modern society values psychopathological behavior before it values natural behaviors, we cannot turn the negative spiral upward again, and we will be every year more paranoid as a metagroup and probably then attract a worldwide fascist tyrant that will embody all the fears, taboos and repressions that we have accumulated as an erotically really stupid culture.

From a sane perspective, it is obvious that giving the child the right for free choice relations is a different agenda than granting political liberty to the cause of pedophilia!

The parallels of the *strategic agenda* of both homosexual and pedophile organizations are striking,

as Jeffrey Satinover convincingly shows in his book. The homosexual cause was political from the start and the research they cited for backing up their claims was produced from their own extended network that is nationwide in the United States.

Satinover retraces their political fight, that was not always transparent and often of an assaulting nature, and that was based on cloning the strategy of Hitler's propaganda minister, Goebbels. It used intimidation to achieve goals. It used to intimidate straight psychiatrists, to get them to trace homosexuality from the DSM, so as to normalize it.

And that was achieved, and much more.

Today we can say that homosexuality is a social force in the United States of America that cannot be overlooked and that pursues their own agenda, which is not necessarily identical with the agenda of the government.

But there is so much economic and thrust power behind them that we can say in a way homosexuals today jointly govern America!

The same can be true tomorrow for the pedophile agenda, despite the obvious reticence today to even discuss this in public. It seems that everybody is

paralyzed to even mention the existence of that attraction, for fear to be drawn into the abyss of ruthless and violently moralistic persecution that has no regard for civil rights, nor for the rights of the child.

So let me be explicit here! The cause I am advocating is the cause of the child, not the cause of pedophilia, which is a cause of a childhood hangup, a *pathology*, as all research, including my own, shows with much evidence.

As homosexuality is not genetic, not hereditary, and not unchangeable, so isn't pedophilia. It is neither genetically predetermined, nor is it hereditary.

And it can be changed, while today, the main bulk of psychiatrists tend to deny this fact, assuming that pedophilia 'cannot be cured.'

I have all the proof to forward the opposite argument, but we have to see that the pedophile witchhunts serve a secret agenda in that they target intellectuals who do not fit in the blindfolding consumerist machinery that this society fosters under the header of 'worldwide democracy' and that it throws over the head of all and every country in the

world that dares to go their own way, and define their own values.

The violence of the *pedophile witchhunt paradigm* is obvious, but it does not for that matter give right to the pedophile cause because such a cause is as fake as the homosexual cause.

The only cause there is, and which is real, is the cause of the child or more precisely, the cause of the sexual child.

I have demonstrated in more than twenty years of research on sexual paraphilias that we all have pedoemotions, but these emotions are caring and tender and they are not by nature sexualized. The biological function of pedoemotions is to ensure that childcare is given enough attention as it ensures the survival of the human race; otherwise we would since long have ceased to exist, as today people care much more about cars, handphones, computers, sumptuous estates and holiday cruises than caring for producing offspring.

This is obvious and shown by statistics!

We are facing more and more female frigidity and besides, a growing interest in consumer goods that is paralleled by a *growing disinterest in having children,*

and bringing up children. For it involves time and care, it involves a good deal of learning also, for the challenge to bring up a sane child in a largely insane culture is obvious.

We are living on the edge, and our choices are open, more open than ever before in human history.

But when we collectively choose to do away with procreation, just for 'enjoying life' and so and so many consumer goods, we are done as a human race!

Hence, the function of *pedoemotions* and why they exist. But my research also shows that pedoemotions are not by nature sexualized, while they may become sexualized for reasons we still ignore.

Sexology doesn't have the answer why in one case pedoemotions do not sexualize and in another case they do.

I have drafted a *teaching tale* to exemplify the complexity of the matter with a practical example. This story shows a male day care teacher, Bernard Farrar, who has been screened and found without blame, who has a stable girlfriend and defines himself as heterosexual, one day engages in sex games with some of the children, for reasons that in the subsequent trial remain largely veiled.

This tale serves as an *empirical fiction* as it is highly probable that many childcare workers will find themselves in said situations.

Therefore, there is an urgent need for additional vocational training for childcare workers which covers unique aspects of care such as pedoemotions, and the building of emotional awareness.

In Bernard's trial, these complex details were not elucidated simply because there was no interest to do so from the side of the authorities who played the 'easy game' as in most such affairs. They simply labeled Bernard a 'pedophile,' having 'sought the access to children in cunning ways,' having absolved his diploma in early child care with the 'premeditated intention to abuse children,' and so on and so forth. The usual rhetoric. But this rhetoric veils the essential, it veils the truth that things like that can happen. It veils the truth that never in human vocational training for teachers the idea came up to *train people who are around children to be emotionally aware,* which means to become vigilantly conscious of their pedoemotions, as I have suggested to implement it as an add-on to vocational training for teachers (with no reaction so far from any professional circles).

Our society seems to be highly afraid of the sexual child, for the simple reason that it assumes that most adults are not ready to face erotically exuberant children without attacking them sexually in one or the other way.

This concern is not far-fetched when one considers my teaching tale. The reason why Bernard interacted sexually with a minority of children in the group, and not all of them was most probably the result of the children having had sensual and sexual feelings for Bernard, in the first place. And Bernard fell into the trap. He became enthralled by the erotic energies of these children, without understanding that these little girls actually projected unconscious incestuous feelings for their fathers upon him. He was trapped by an attraction he could not cognize, and as he had never received formal training on these matters, he became a victim of a situation he was not equipped to handle.

Of course, in the legal setting, he was labeled as a child predator, whose chief aim was to satisfy his huge ego needs and lust for forbidden fruits, as the prosecutor poetically termed it in his philippic.

In truth, Bernard did not have the faintest idea of such a thing when he started out to become an educator. He had never even once thought about such a thing, and he would have quite decidedly rejected such an idea, as a matter of his professional ethics.

All those group fantasies were thus projected upon him, by the media, by the metagroup that needs scapegoats for their derelict repressed perversions. And the media rejoiced, more than anybody else involved in that sordid trial, about all the stories it could invent around the 'perpetrator' that needed to be 'crushed' by law enforcement, and who was feeling that the entire world was collapsing on his head and shoulders.

In a climate of paranoid fear and terror as it is reality today in postmodern consumer cultures around the world, no more true education can be done. It is a fact that educators who never had training for handling pedoemotions cannot responsibly cope with the pressures and psychic tension which is the reason for the increase in teachers committing suicide for allegedly 'unknown reasons.'

It is also the reason for youngsters attacking teachers violently which is a growing concern

especially in France where many teachers have been murdered by their students, in schools all over the country, and for which the government largely has no explanation.

Nicola Sarkozy's approach to handling pedophilia in French society is notoriously a combative one, and as such, treats a certain sexual minority group in an uncivilized fashion.

His approach was during his presidency in accord with global paranoia regarding the issue of pedophilia.

But Mr. Sarkozy should recognize that France is a pluralistic society like many other countries and as such, sexual diversities do exist and must be acknowledged and respected through due process. His proposal to eradicate members of the said group via euthanasia, in which lethal medical drugs are administered with the chief aim of ending someone's life, constitutes uncivilized policy-making. This proposed approach to the handling of pedophilia can be seen as an attempt to *sexually cleanse France of people deemed as demons* in much the same way as he demonizes the Muslim immigrants residing in France.

That is why social change is needed for we cannot allow Nazi-like behavior to surface once again. Permissive education entails showing the entire picture and not just part of it or a distorted one. The reasons for this polemic are obviously political. Sarkozy made the game easy when he blamed 'pedophiles' for all the pitfalls of his largely *incompetent presidency* and his *inability to communicate effectively with groups,* let alone integrate different interest groups politically and socially.

In addition, he seems to be obsessed by the idea that pedophilia was 'inborn and unchangeable' and that for that reason, pedophiles have to be euthanized.

It's really a fascist agenda as we know it from the times of Hitler and Mussolini and in Italy it was at the time exactly the same, under Berlusconi. Hence, the political explosiveness of the subject but also why both these fascist rulers were chased by their politically conscious populations!

If children are not allowed to be sexual, and to have free choice relations, there is only one argument why this is denied. This one single argument is that our leaders are insane! Police terror was largely rising

in France and Italy under Sarkozy and Berlusconi exactly for these reasons, and the cause of the child was treaded in the gutter. Children were streamlined to ideological ideas and political strategies just as under any fascist and totalitarian regime of the past. Fortunately this tragic comedy of corrupt leadership was ended by the political will of the peoples!

In this context it is of course highly disturbing for political leaders to learn from cutting-edge research that children are erotically conscious and have real sexual feelings, not just 'autoerotic' desires as Freud and the rest of Freudian psychoanalysis tends to assume.

We know today through multiple pathways of research that children are not just autoerotic, but fully erotic in the sense that they desire to have complete intercourse as early as possible with partners of their choice. This fact is demonstrated in children's sometimes playful behavior in which they try to imitate sexual intercourse by thrusting their pelvis while laughing—an activity often done by male children.

The changes of legal and social policy that I am suggesting here are obvious when one really peruses my reasoning and the scientific data that back it up.

These changes must be *thorough and radical* or they will not bring any significant change for the better. In clear text, this means a total abolishment of all sex laws, the decriminalization of all human sexual behavior, and the establishment of trusted consultancy consisting of trained psychiatric personnel specifically engaged to provide counsel to people thereby ensuring they are able to handle their vital energies constructively. By contrast, to give way to the pedophile movement's claims for recognition would lead to a similar situation as it is now with homosexuality, where a social grouping maintains power as it were 'on false premises' because the scientific data that is advanced to backup its 'natural' attraction, are for the most part truncated.

Such a 'normalization' of pedophilia would not necessarily bring any advantage for children; it would not per se give the child free choice relations. Social policy making must start not from a utopian or far-fetched agenda, but from the status quo! The status quo regarding children's rights is such that the child in the modern nuclear family cannot really

Proposal 12/12

It seems to me that the widely irrational and aggressive polemics against pedophilia in our mass media have very specific reasons. First of all, it has nothing to do with morality. Second, it has nothing to do with child protection. Third, it has much to do with veiling the state of the art, or rather, the state of the lacking art of our modern education. It has much to do with covering up the *deplorable ignorance* we have in front of children's full humanity, and the equally *deplorable arrogance* we hold on to when we regard them as pleasure cuties and night pillows for their emotionally immature parents.

This cover-up function of the pedophilia polemics becomes obvious when one has done large-scale research on the reasons why men and women choose children as their partners, through deliberate emotional choice and a resulting sexual attraction in some of the cases. I stress the fact that the sexual attraction is indeed second, and that it is random, as we do not yet know why natural pedoemotions turn sexual in one case, but not in another case.

For example, it is known that the British mathematician and photographer Lewis Carroll loved

little girls, but it is not known if he was in any way also sexually attracted to them. For the least we do not have any evidence to the latter assumption. This is what I call an 'emotional predilection.'

But of course, the whole of the myth of the pedophile predator covers up the fact that pedoemotions are natural because they are at the basis of our interest to procreate, and also our interest to become teachers or day care workers. When a person says 'I love children' one does regularly not associate that the person is sexually attracted to children. One associates that the person has an emotional predilection for children, which means an interest in being around children, an interest also to care for children, and sometimes an interest to save children from any unfortunate life circumstances, which includes, for example, the desire to become a nurse in a pediatrics hospital or to work for an NGO that works for improving the life conditions of children in the third world or in countries where there is war or civil war.

Yet the perhaps astonishing fact is that it is often within these professions that adult-child sexual contacts happen and are found out. This was quite obvious also when the persecution of child sex

offenders started in the Philippines and Sri Lanka, in the 1980s. Many of those arrested child sex tourists turned out to be child care workers, teachers and pediatricians.

This shows that regularly, a sexual attraction develops as it were on top of a *prevalent emotional predilection*. This insight is the result of my own research; it is nowhere to be found in books on child abuse, nor in sexology manuals, for the simple reason that today's mental health professionals still assume that human sexuality was a 'drive', that is, an automatism. But it is not, not at all.

The assumption of 'sexual drives' was first made by Sigmund Freud and it was harshly contradicted by Wilhelm Reich who wrote this in one of his books:

> I stress the rationality of the primary emotions of all living. The mechanists of depth psychology have namely spread the view that all emotions were but drives and therefore irrational. However, emotions are specific functions of the protoplasm. Emotions and the natural movement of the bioplasm are functionally identical phenomena.

As Dr. Reich said it, the Freudian view and the view of modern sexology regarding the human sexual function is completely and hopelessly mechanistic. It

is wrong because the human being, as modern science discovered through the systems view of life, is not a machine!

Now, how to draft a social policy that both makes for happier childhoods and that avoids people turning into homosexuals and pedophiles?

The way to go is to draft an *educational agenda* that is the most possible respectful toward the emotional and sexual needs of the child and to change our 'public morals' accordingly.

The above-mentioned policy proposal will most likely be difficult to embrace by most people for it is radical in vision; hence the need for a definite break from mainstream thinking.

However, I harbor a sense of urgency here and the rest of the world should, too, if we are to foster a more pro-life future.

In order to activate social change for the betterment of everybody, the only way to bring about social change which takes into account the greatest happiness for the greatest number is to introduce social and legal suggestions *aimed at reducing violence and paranoia,* while at the same time gradually

developing a more pleasure oriented, pro-sexual society.

With the current polemics and the church-driven propaganda against sexual diversity, what we create is more of violence, more of homosexuality and more of pedophilia. It's as simple as that. But this is not what we want as a sane society, right?

So we should give reasonably course to a liberation of the child from consumer pressure, and allow children *free choice relations* within the realm of natural morality, which means that children learn to respect the golden rule of conduct, that is, to do no harm to self and others!

Bibliography

Contextual Bibliography

Abrams, Jeremiah (Ed.)
Reclaiming the Inner Child
New York: Tarcher/Putnam, 1990

Appleton, Matthew
A Free Range Childhood
Self-Regulation at Summerhill School
Foundation for Educational Renewal, 2000

Summerhill
Kindern ihre Kindheit zurückgeben
Demokratie und Selbstregulierung in der Erziehung
Hohengehren: Schneider Verlag, 2003

Alston, John P. / Tucker, Francis
The Myth of Sexual Permissiveness
The Journal of Sex Research, 9/1 (1973)

Ariès, Philippe
L'enfant et la famille sous l'Ancien Régime
Paris, Seuil, 1975

Centuries of Childhood
New York: Vintage Books, 1962

Geschichte der Kindheit
Frankfurt/M: DTV, 1998

Bachofen, Johann Jakob
Das Mutterrecht
Basel: Benno Schwabe & Co., 1948
Gesammelte Werke, Band II
Erstveröffentlichung im Jahre 1861

Barbaree, Howard E. & Marshall, William L. (Eds.)

The Juvenile Sex Offender
Second Edition
New York: Guilford Press, 2008

Bertalanffy, Ludwig von

General Systems Theory
Foundations, Development, Applications
New York: George Brazilier Publishing, 1976

Bettelheim, Bruno

A Good Enough Parent
New York: A. Knopf, 1987

The Uses of Enchantment
New York: Vintage Books, 1989

Kinder brauchen Märchen
Frankfurt/M: DTV, 2002

Boadalla, David

Wilhelm Reich, Leben und Werk
Frankfurt/M: Fischer, 1980

Böhm, Wilfried

Maria Montessori
2. Auflage
Bad Heilbrunn: Julius Klinkhardt, 1991

Bohm, David

Wholeness and the Implicate Order
London: Routledge, 2002

Bordeaux-Szekely, Edmond

Teaching of the Essenes from Enoch to the Dead Sea Scrolls
Beekman Publishing, 1992

Gospel of the Essenes
The Unknown Books of the Essenes
& Lost Scrolls of the Essene Brotherhood
Beekman Publishing, 1988

Gospel of Peace of Jesus Christ
Beekman Publishing, 1994

Brennan, Barbara Ann

Hands of Healing
A Guide to Healing Through the Human Energy Field
New York: Bantam, 1988

Bullough & Bullough (Eds.)

Human Sexuality
An Encyclopedia
New York: Garland Publishing, 1994

Sin, Sickness and Sanity
A History of Sexual Attitudes
New York: New American Library, 1977

Cain, Chelsea & Moon Unit Zappa

Wild Child
New York: Seal Press (Feminist Publishing), 1999

Calderone & Ramey

Talking With Your Child About Sex
New York: Random House, 1982

Capra, Fritjof

The Turning Point
Science, Society And The Rising Culture
New York: Simon & Schuster, 1987
Original Author Copyright, 1982

Wendezeit
Bausteine für ein neues Weltbild
München: Droemer Knaur, 2004

Le temps du changement
Science, société et nouvelle culture
Paris: Rocher, 1994

The Tao of Physics
An Exploration of the Parallels Between Modern
Physics and Eastern Mysticism
New York: Shambhala Publications, 2000
(New Edition) Originally published in 1975

Das Tao der Physik
Die Konvergenz von westlicher Wissenschaft und östlicher Philosophie
Neue und erweiterte Auflage
München: O.W. Barth bei Scherz, 2000

The Web of Life
A New Scientific Understanding of Living Systems
New York: Doubleday, 1997
Author Copyright 1996

The Hidden Connections
Integrating The Biological, Cognitive And Social
Dimensions Of Life Into A Science Of Sustainability
New York: Doubleday, 2002

Steering Business Toward Sustainability
New York: United Nations University Press, 1995

Uncommon Wisdom
Conversations with Remarkable People
New York: Bantam, 1989

The Science of Leonardo
Inside the Mind of the Great Genius of the Renaissance
New York: Anchor Books, 2008
New York: Bantam Doubleday, 2007 (First Publishing)

Cho, Susanne

Kindheit und Sexualität im Wandel der Kulturgeschichte
Eine Studie zur Bedeutung der kindlichen Sexualität unter besonderer
Berücksichtigung des 17. und 20. Jahrhunderts
Zürich, 1983 (Doctoral thesis)

Constantine, Larry L.

Children & Sex
New Findings, New Perspectives
Larry L. Constantine & Floyd M. Martinson (Eds.)
Boston: Little, Brown & Company, 1981

Treasures of the Island
Children in Alternative Lifestyles
Beverly Hills: Sage Publications, 1976

Where are the Kids?
in: Libby & Whitehurst (ed.)
Marriage and Alternatives
Glenview: Scott Foresman, 1977

Open Family
A Lifestyle for Kids and other People
26 FAMILY COORDINATOR 113-130 (1977)

Covitz, Joel

Emotional Child Abuse
The Family Curse
Boston: Sigo Press, 1986

Currier, Richard L.

Juvenile Sexuality in Global Perspective
in : Children & Sex, New Findings, New Perspectives
Larry L. Constantine & Floyd M. Martinson (Eds.)
Boston: Little, Brown & Company, 1981

DiCarlo, Russell E. (Ed.)

Towards A New World View
Conversations at the Leading Edge
Erie, PA: Epic Publishing, 1996

Dolto, Françoise

La Cause des Enfants
Paris: Laffont, 1985

Psychanalyse et Pédiatrie
Paris: Seuil, 1971

Séminaire de Psychanalyse d'Enfants, 1
Paris: Seuil, 1982

Séminaire de Psychanalyse d'Enfants, 2
Paris: Seuil, 1985

Séminaire de Psychanalyse d'Enfants, 3
Paris: Seuil, 1988

L'évangile au risque de la psychanalyse
Paris: Seuil, 1980

Eden, Donna & Feinstein, David

Energy Medicine
New York: Tarcher/Putnam, 1998

The Energy Medicine Kit
Simple Effective Techniques to Help You Boost Your Vitality
Boulder, Co.: Sounds True Editions, 2004

The Promise of Energy Psychology
With David Feinstein and Gary Craig
Revolutionary Tools for Dramatic Personal Change
New York: Jeremy P. Tarcher/Penguin, 2005

Ellis, Havelock

Sexual Inversion
Republished
New York: University Press of the Pacific, 2001
Originally published in 1897

Elwin, V.

The Muria and their Ghotul
Bombay: Oxford University Press, 1947

Emoto, Masaru

The Hidden Messages in Water
New York: Atria Books, 2004

The Secret Life of Water
New York: Atria Books, 2005

Erikson, Erik H.

Childhood and Society
New York: Norton, 1993
First published in 1950

Erman/Ranke

Ägypten und Ägyptisches Leben im Altertum
Hildesheim: Gerstenberg, 1981

Foster/Freed

A Bill of Rights for Children
6 FAMILY LAW QUARTERLY 343 (1972)

Foucault, Michel

The History of Sexuality, Vol. I : The Will to Knowledge
London: Penguin, 1998
First published in 1976

The History of Sexuality, Vol. II : The Use of Pleasure
London: Penguin, 1998
First published in 1984

The History of Sexuality, Vol. III : The Care of Self
London: Penguin, 1998
First published in 1984

BIBLIOGRAPHY

Freud, Anna

War and Children
London: 1943

Freud, Sigmund

Three Essays on the Theory of Sexuality
in: The Standard Edition of the Complete Psychological Works of
Sigmund Freud, London: Hogarth Press, 1953-54, Vol. 7, pp. 130 ff.
(first published in 1905)

The Interpretation of Dreams
New York: Avon, Reissue Edition, 1980
and in: The Standard Edition of the Complete Works of Sigmund Freud
(24 Volumes) ed. by James Strachey
New York: W. W. Norton & Company, 1976

Totem and Taboo
New York: Routledge, 1999
Originally published in 1913

Fromm, Erich

The Anatomy of Human Destructiveness
New York: Owl Book, 1992
Originally published in 1973

Gerber, Richard

A Practical Guide to Vibrational Medicine
Energy Healing and Spiritual Transformation
New York: Harper & Collins, 2001

Gil, David G.

Societal Violence and Violence in Families
in: David G. Gil, Child Abuse and Violence
New York: Ams Press, 1928

Goleman, Daniel

Emotional Intelligence
New York, Bantam Books, 1995

Grof, Stanislav

Ancient Wisdom and Modern Science
New York: State University of New York Press, 1984

Beyond the Brain
Birth, Death and Transcendence in Psychotherapy
New York: State University of New York, 1985

Realms of the Human Unconscious
Observations from LSD Research
New York: E.P. Dutton, 1976

The Cosmic Game
Explorations of the Frontiers of Human Consciousness
New York: State University of New York Press, 1998

The Holotropic Mind
The Three Levels of Human Consciousness
With Hal Zina Bennett
New York: HarperCollins, 1993

When the Impossible Happens
Adventures in Non-Ordinary Reality
Louisville, CO: Sounds True, 2005

Groth, A. Nicholas

Men Who Rape
The Psychology of the Offender
New York: Perseus Publishing, 1980

Houston, Jean

The Possible Human
A Course in Enhancing Your Physical, Mental, and Creative Abilities
New York: Jeremy P. Tarcher/Putnam, 1982

Howells, Kevin

Adult Sexual Interest in Children
Considerations Relevant to Theories of Aetiology in:
Cook, M. and Howells, K. (eds.): Adult Sexual Interest in Children
Academic Press, London, 1980

Jackson, Stevi

Childhood and Sexuality
New York: Blackwell, 1982

Jung, Carl Gustav

Archetypes of the Collective Unconscious
in: The Basic Writings of C.G. Jung
New York: The Modern Library, 1959, 358-407

Collected Works
New York, 1959

On the Nature of the Psyche
in: The Basic Writings of C.G. Jung
New York: The Modern Library, 1959, 47-133

Psychological Types
Collected Writings, Vol. 6
Princeton: Princeton University Press, 1971

Psychology and Religion
in: The Basic Writings of C.G. Jung
New York: The Modern Library, 1959, 582-655

Religious and Psychological Problems of Alchemy
in: The Basic Writings of C.G. Jung
New York: The Modern Library, 1959, 537-581

The Basic Writings of C.G. Jung
New York: The Modern Library, 1959

The Development of Personality
Collected Writings, Vol. 17
Princeton: Princeton University Press, 1954

The Meaning and Significance of Dreams
Boston: Sigo Press, 1991

The Myth of the Divine Child
in: Essays on A Science of Mythology
Princeton, N.J.: Princeton University Press Bollingen
Series XXII, 1969. (With Karl Kerenyi)

Two Essays on Analytical Psychology
Collected Writings, Vol. 7
Princeton: Princeton University Press, 1972
First published by Routledge & Kegan Paul, Ltd., 1953

Karagulla, Shafica

The Chakras
Correlations between Medical Science and Clairvoyant Observation
With Dora van Gelder Kunz
Wheaton: Quest Books, 1989

Kerner, Justinus

F.A. Mesmer aus Schwaben
Frankfurt/M, 1856

Kiesewetter, Carl

Franz Anton Mesmer's Leben und Lehre
Leipzig, 1893

Klein, Melanie

Love, Guilt and Reparation, and Other Works 1921-1945
New York: Free Press, 1984
(Reissue Edition)

Envy and Gratitude and Other Works 1946-1963
New York: Free Press, 2002
(Reissue Edition)

Krafft-Ebing, Richard von

Psychopathia sexualis
New York: Bell Publishing, 1965
Originally published in 1886

Krishnamurti, J.

Freedom From The Known
San Francisco: Harper & Row, 1969

The First and Last Freedom
San Francisco: Harper & Row, 1975

Education and the Significance of Life
London: Victor Gollancz, 1978

Commentaries on Living
First Series
London: Victor Gollancz, 1985

Commentaries on Living
Second Series
London: Victor Gollancz, 1986

Krishnamurti's Journal
London: Victor Gollancz, 1987

Krishnamurti's Notebook
London: Victor Gollancz, 1986

Beyond Violence
London: Victor Gollancz, 1985

Beginnings of Learning
New York: Penguin, 1986

The Penguin Krishnamurti Reader
New York: Penguin, 1987

On God
San Francisco: Harper & Row, 1992

On Fear
San Francisco: Harper & Row, 1995

The Essential Krishnamurti
San Francisco: Harper & Row, 1996

The Ending of Time
With Dr. David Bohm
San Francisco: Harper & Row, 1985

Laing, Ronald David

Divided Self
New York: Viking Press, 1991

R.D. Laing and the Paths of Anti-Psychiatry
ed., by Z. Kotowicz
London: Routledge, 1997

The Politics of Experience
New York: Pantheon, 1983

Lakhovsky, Georges

La Science et le Bonheur
Longévité et Immortalité par les Vibrations
Paris: Gauthier-Villars, 1930

Le Secret de la Vie
Paris: Gauthier-Villars, 1929

Secret of Life
New York: Kessinger Publishing, 2003

L'étiologie du Cancer
Paris: Gauthier-Villars, 1929

L'Universion
Paris: Gauthier-Villars, 1927

Laszlo, Ervin

Science and the Akashic Field
An Integral Theory of Everything
Rochester: Inner Traditions, 2004

Quantum Shift to the Global Brain
How the New Scientific Reality Can Change Us and Our World
Rochester: Inner Traditions, 2008

Science and the Reenchantment of the Cosmos
The Rise of the Integral Vision of Reality
Rochester: Inner Traditions, 2006

The Akashic Experience
Science and the Cosmic Memory Field
Rochester: Inner Traditions, 2009

The Chaos Point
The World at the Crossroads
Newburyport, MA: Hampton Roads Publishing, 2006

Laud, Anne & Gilstrop, May

Violence in the Family
A Selected Bibliography on Child Abuse, Sexual Abuse of Children &
Domestic Violence, June 1985, University of Georgia Libraries
Bibliographical Series, No. 32

Leboyer, Frederick

Birth Without Violence
New York, 1975

Pour une Naissance sans Violence
Paris: Seuil, 1974

Cette Lumière d'où vient l'Enfant
Paris: Seuil, 1978

Inner Beauty, Inner Light
New York: Newmarket Press, 1997

Loving Hands
The Traditional Art of Baby Massage
New York: Newmarket Press, 1977

The Art of Breathing
New York: Newmarket Press, 1991

Leonard, George, Murphy, Michael

The Live We Are Given
A Long Term Program for Realizing the
Potential of Body, Mind, Heart and Soul
New York: Jeremy P. Tarcher/Putnam, 1984

Liedloff, Jean

Continuum Concept
In Search of Happiness Lost
New York: Perseus Books, 1986
First published in 1977

Auf der Suche nach dem verlorenen Glück
Gegen die Zerstörung der Glücksfähigkeit in der frühen Kindheit
München: C.H. Beck Verlag, 2006

Lipton, Bruce

The Biology of Belief
Unleashing the Power of Consciousness, Matter and Miracles
Santa Rosa, CA: Mountain of Love / Elite Books, 2005

Locke, John

Some Thoughts Concerning Education
London, 1690
Reprinted in: The Works of John Locke, 1823
Vol. IX., pp. 6-205

Long, Max *Freedom*

The Secret Science at Work
The Huna Method as a Way of Life
Marina del Rey: De Vorss Publications, 1995
Originally published in 1953

Growing Into Light
A Personal Guide to Practicing the Huna Method,
Marina del Rey: De Vorss Publications, 1955

Lowen, Alexander

Bioenergetics
New York: Coward, McGoegham 1975

Depression and the Body
The Biological Basis of Faith and Reality
New York: Penguin, 1992

Fear of Life
New York: Bioenergetic Press, 2003

Honoring the Body
The Autobiography of Alexander Lowen
New York: Bioenergetic Press, 2004

Joy
The Surrender to the Body and to Life
New York: Penguin, 1995

Love and Orgasm
New York: Macmillan, 1965

Love, Sex and Your Heart
New York: Bioenergetics Press, 2004

Narcissism: Denial of the True Self
New York: Macmillan, Collier Books, 1983

Pleasure: A Creative Approach to Life
New York: Bioenergetics Press, 2004
First published in 1970

The Language of the Body
Physical Dynamics of Character Structure
New York: Bioenergetics Press, 2006 (First published in 1958)

Malinowski, Bronislaw

Crime und Custom in Savage Society
London: Kegan, 1926

Sex and Repression in Savage Society
London: Kegan, 1927

The Sexual Life of Savages in North West Melanesia
New York: Halcyon House, 1929

Mann, Edward W.

Orgone, Reich & Eros
Wilhelm Reich's Theory of Life Energy
New York: Simon & Schuster (Touchstone), 1973

Martinson, Floyd M.

Sexual Knowledge
Values and Behavior Patterns
St. Peter: Minn.: Gustavus Adolphus College, 1966

Infant and Child Sexuality
St. Peter: Minn.: Gustavus Adolphus College, 1973

The Quality of Adolescent Experiences
St. Peter: Minn.: Gustavus Adolphus College, 1974

The Child and the Family
Calgary, Alberta: The University of Calgary, 1980

The Sex Education of Young Children
in: Lorna Brown (Ed.), *Sex Education in the Eighties*
New York, London: Plenum Press, 1981, pp. 51 ff.

The Sexual Life of Children
New York: Bergin & Garvey, 1994

McTaggart, Lynne

The Field
The Quest for the Secret Force of the Universe
New York: Harper & Collins, 2002

Mead, Margaret

Sex and Temperament in Three Primitive Societies
New York, 1935

Miller, Alice

Four Your Own Good
Hidden Cruelty in Child-Rearing and the Roots of Violence
New York: Farrar, Straus & Giroux, 1983

The Drama of the Gifted Child
In Search for the True Self
translated by Ruth Ward
New York: Basic Books, 1996

Thou Shalt Not Be Aware
Society's Betrayal of the Child
New York: Noonday, 1998

The Political Consequences of Child Abuse
in: The Journal of Psychohistory 26, 2 (Fall 1998)

Moll, Albert

The Sexual Life of the Child
New York: Macmillan, 1912
First published in German as
Das Sexualleben des Kindes, 1909

Montagu, Ashley

Touching
The Human Significance of the Skin
New York: Harper & Row, 1978

Montessori, Maria

The Absorbent Mind
Reprint Edition
New York: Buccaneer Books, 1995
First published in 1973

Moser, Charles Allen

DSM-IV-TR and the Paraphilias: an argument for removal
With Peggy J. Kleinplatz
Journal of Psychology and Human Sexuality 17 (3/4), 91-109 (2005)

Murdock, G.

Social Structure
New York: Macmillan, 1960

Myss, Caroline

The Creation of Health
The Emotional, Psychological, and Spiritual Responses that Promote
Health and Healing
New York: Three Rivers Press, 1998

Nau, Erika

Self-Awareness Through Huna
Virginia Beach: Donning, 1981

Neill, Alexander Sutherland

Neill! Neill! Orange-Peel!
New York: Hart Publishing Co., 1972

Summerhill
A Radical Approach to Child Rearing
New York: Hart Publishing, Reprint 1984
Originally published 1960

Summerhill School
A New View of Childhood
New York: St. Martin's Press
Reprint 1995

Neumann, Erich

The Great Mother
Princeton: Princeton University Press, 1955
(Bollingen Series)

Odent, Michel

Birth Reborn
What Childbirth Should Be
London: Souvenir Press, 1994

The Scientification of Love
London: Free Association Books, 1999

Primal Health
Understanding the Critical Period Between Conception and the First Birthday
London: Clairview Books, 2002
First Published in 1986 with Century Hutchinson in London

The Functions of the Orgasms
The Highway to Transcendence
London: Pinter & Martin, 2009

Ollendorf-Reich, Ilse

Wilhelm Reich, A Personal Biography
New York, St. Martins Press, 1969

Pert, Candace B.

Molecules of Emotion
The Science Behind Mind-Body Medicine
New York: Scribner, 2003

Porteous, Hedy S.

Sex and Identity
Your Child's Sexuality
Indianapolis: Bobbs-Merrill, 1972

Prescott, James W.

Affectional Bonding for the Prevention of Violent Behaviors
Neurobiological, Psychological and Religious/Spiritual Determinants
in: Hertzberg, L.J., Ostrum, G.F. and Field, J.R., (Eds.)
Violent Behavior
Vol. 1, Assessment & Intervention, Chapter Six
New York: PMA Publishing, 1990

Alienation of Affection
Psychology Today, December 1979

Body Pleasure and the Origins of Violence
Bulletin of the Atomic Scientists, 10-20 (1975)

Deprivation of Physical Affection as a Primary Process in the Development of Physical Violence A Comparative and Cross-Cultural Perspective, in: David G. Gil, ed., Child Abuse and Violence
New York: Ams Press, 1979

Raknes, Ola

Wilhelm Reich and Orgonomy
Oslo: Universitetsforlaget, 1970

Reich, Wilhelm

A Review of the Theories, dating from The 17th Century, on the Origin of Organic Life, by Arthur Hahn, Literature Assistant at the Institut für Sexualökonomische Lebensforschung, Biologisches Laboratorium, Oslo, 1938
©1979 by Mary Boyd Higgins as Director of the Wilhelm Reich Infant Trust, XEROX Copy from the Wilhelm Reich Museum

Children of the Future
On the Prevention of Sexual Pathology
New York: Farrar, Straus & Giroux, 1983
First published in 1950

CORE (Cosmic Orgone Engineering)
Part I, Space Ships, DOR and DROUGHT
©1984, Orgone Institute Press
XEROX Copy from the Wilhelm Reich Museum

Early Writings 1
New York: Farrar, Straus & Giroux, 1975

Ether, God & Devil & Cosmic Superimposition
New York: Farrar, Straus & Giroux, 1972
Originally published in 1949

Genitality in the Theory and Therapy of Neurosis
©1980 by Mary Boyd Higgins as Director of the Wilhelm Reich Infant Trust

People in Trouble
©1974 by Mary Boyd Higgins as Director of the Wilhelm Reich Infant Trust

Record of a Friendship
The Correspondence of Wilhelm Reich and A. S. Neill
New York, Farrar, Straus & Giroux, 1981

Selected Writings
An Introduction to Orgonomy
New York: Farrar, Straus & Giroux, 1973

The Bioelectrical Investigation of Sexuality and Anxiety
New York: Farrar, Straus & Giroux, 1983
Originally published in 1935

The Bion Experiments
reprinted in *Selected Writings*
New York: Farrar, Straus & Giroux, 1973

The Cancer Biopathy (The Orgone, Vol. 2)
New York: Farrar, Straus & Giroux, 1973

The Function of the Orgasm (The Orgone, Vol. 1)
Orgone Institute Press, New York, 1942

The Invasion of Compulsory Sex Morality
New York: Farrar, Straus & Giroux, 1971
Originally published in 1932

The Leukemia Problem: Approach
©1951, Orgone Institute Press
Copyright Renewed 1979
XEROX Copy from the Wilhelm Reich Museum

The Mass Psychology of Fascism
New York: Farrar, Straus & Giroux, 1970
Originally published in 1933

The Orgone Energy Accumulator
Its Scientific and Medical Use
©1951, 1979, Orgone Institute Press
XEROX Copy from the Wilhelm Reich Museum

The Schizophrenic Split
©1945, 1949, 1972 by Mary Boyd Higgins as Director of the
Wilhelm Reich Infant Trust
XEROX Copy from the Wilhelm Reich Museum

The Sexual Revolution
©1945, 1962 by Mary Boyd Higgins as Director of the Wilhelm Reich
Infant Trust

Reid, Daniel P.

The Tao of Health, Sex & Longevity
A Modern Practical Guide to the Ancient Way
New York: Simon & Schuster, 1989

Guarding the Three Treasures
The Chinese Way of Health
New York: Simon & Schuster, 1993

Rothschild & Wolf

Children of the Counterculture
New York: Garden City, 1976

Satinover, Jeffrey

Homosexuality and the Politics of Truth
New York: Baker Books, 1996

Sharaf, Myron

Fury on Earth
A Biography of Wilhelm Reich
London: André Deutsch, 1983

Sheldrake, Rupert

A New Science of Life
The Hypothesis of Morphic Resonance
Rochester: Park Street Press, 1995

Singer, June

Androgyny
New York: Doubleday Dell, 1976

Stekel, Wilhelm

Auto-Eroticism
A Psychiatric Study of Onanism and Neurosis
Republished, London: Paul Kegan, 2004

Patterns of Psychosexual Infantilism
New York, 1959 (reprint edition)

Sadism and Masochism
New York: W.W. Norton & Co., 1953

Sex and Dreams
The Language of Dreams
Republished
New York: University Press of the Pacific, 2003

Stone, Hal & Stone, Sidra

Embracing Our Selves
The Voice Dialogue Manual
San Rafael, CA: New World Library, 1989

Tischner, Rudolf

F.A. Mesmer
München, 1928

Villoldo, Alberto

Healing States
A Journey Into the World of Spiritual Healing and Shamanism
With Stanley Krippner
New York: Simon & Schuster (Fireside), 1987

The Four Insights
Wisdom, Power, and Grace of the Earthkeepers
New York: Hay House, 2006

Shaman, Healer, Sage
How to Heal Yourself and Others with the Energy Medicine of the
Americas
New York: Harmony, 2000

Healing the Luminous Body
The Way of the Shaman with Dr. Alberto Villoldo
DVD, Sacred Mysteries Productions, 2004

Mending The Past And Healing The Future with Soul Retrieval
New York: Hay House, 2005

Whiting, Beatrice B.

Children of Six Cultures
A Psycho-Cultural Analysis
Cambridge: Harvard University Press, 1975

Williams, Strephon Kaplan

Dreams and Spiritual Growth
With Patricia H. Berne and Louis M. Savary
New York: Paulist Press, 1984

Dream Cards
Understand Your Dreams and Enrich Your Life
New York: Simon & Schuster (Fireside), 1991

Yates, Alayne

Sex Without Shame
Encouraging the Child's Healthy Sexual Development
New York, 1978
Republished Internet Edition

Personal Notes

www.ingramcontent.com/pod-product-compliance
Lightning Source LLC
Chambersburg PA
CBHW030428290526
45786CB00001B/182